A LITTLE LIGHT ✳ ON THE ✳ SPIRITUAL LAWS

✳

ALSO BY DIANA COOPER

A Little Light on Ascension
A Little Light on Angels
Golden Footsteps
(*published by Findhorn Press*)

Light Up Your Life
A Time for Transformation
Transform Your Life
The Power of Inner Peace
(*published by Piatkus*)

DIANA COOPER

A
LITTLE
LIGHT
ON THE
SPIRITUAL
LAWS

This book offers you the keys
 to heaven

Hodder & Stoughton

Copyright © 2000 by Diana Cooper

First published in Great Britain in 2000 by Hodder and Stoughton
A division of Hodder Headline

20

A CIP catalogue record for this title is available from the
British Library

ISBN 0 340 76863 0

Typeset by Palimpsest Book Production Limited,
Polmont, Stirlingshire
Printed and bound in Great Britain by
Clays Ltd, St Ives plc

Hodder and Stoughton
A division of Hodder Headline
338 Euston Road
London NW1 3BH

✷ CONTENTS ✷

THE LAWS OF HIGHER AWARENESS

THE LAWS OF HIGHER FREQUENCY

INTRODUCTION

Life on Earth is a team game. It is vital to learn the rules so that you can participate and make your contribution. A game of football would become a free-for-all if everyone did their own thing, so players are taught the rules before they go on to the field. In the same way we are taught the spiritual laws before we are born. When you understand and follow the spiritual laws you can create heaven on Earth. But life on Earth has turned into a free-for-all because people have forgotten them or chosen to disregard them.

This book offers reminders and an understanding of the spiritual laws.

For thousands of years humans have played the game like a rabble of children. Relationships have been based on need and desire for control, success measured by material gain and possessions. Predominant emotions have been anger, hurt and fear because people have been focused on physical and sexual sensation.

When people take themselves too seriously they are critical and judgmental of themselves and others. Many feel tense and out of control. Often people feel they have to justify their existence or prove their superiority, so that life becomes a power struggle and disharmony prevails.

That is the old paradigm for life on Earth.

It is time for change. Divine discontent is entering people's hearts. The mass consciousness on Earth is changing so that people are no longer satisfied with need and greed. We want a better way of living. To achieve this we are asked to learn the rules, work together and clean up our game. We are preparing for promotion to a higher league.

Collectively we are in the process of moving to a higher dimension. Old habits and unresolved issues are surfacing so that they can be examined and released to make way for the new. Social structures are beginning to collapse. Monarchies, parliaments, big business, banks and all dinosaur institutions are moving towards change or extinction. Some wars are similar to boils: anger has festered into hostility and is now being cleared out like pus.

Many now, through hard work, co-operation and discipline, have reached the top league. They are playing in the cup final with the eyes of the world on them and providing inspiration for all. When you reach this level do not worry about those still disregarding the rules. Be an example of how the game can be played.

When we follow the spiritual laws we are able to reach enlightenment. We experience a feeling of oneness and live in love, compassion and trust. We become masters, following our own guidance and not allowing ourselves to be deflected by anyone else. Our greatest joy is to serve humanity and the Universe.

This is heaven on Earth. Life becomes joyous, peaceful and harmonious. We co-operate with and empower others. We let go of our ego desires and live for the Divine.

Earth is a plane of free will. We can choose whether or not to follow the laws. However, we reap the rewards if we do and bear the consequences if we do not.

People often ask how much free choice we actually have and how much is inevitable. Your Higher Self makes certain decisions before you come to Earth. Your soul makes these choices based on the experiences you need for your progress. You may choose to be born to difficult parents because they embody the challenge your soul needs. While you might reject this as ludicrous your soul views your life from a greater perspective. You may meet the person you will marry because you have karma to repay or because you have earned the right to happiness together. You may have a child who dies because your soul needs to experience loss. Your life may be totally disrupted when you are thirty by unexpected events.

These are pre-life decisions which are inevitable. But you have free choice about how you handle each of these circumstances and can make decisions about everything else in your life. It is rather like buying a round-the-world ticket. There are certain stopovers and pre-booked flights that you agree before you set off. What you do the rest of the time is up to you.

As you follow the spiritual laws and raise your game, your mission here is revealed to you. When you have a vision of what you intend to accomplish during your journey on Earth your clarity and purpose fill you with joy.

We are preparing for the year 2012 or thereabouts when there will be a mass awakening of human consciousness. A quantum leap is to take place.

Once in every ten million years, there is a moment of stillness, a moment of total silence in the Universe. At that moment changes take place that are beyond our comprehension. We have absolutely no concept of the enormity of what awaits us at that moment.

The calendar of the Mayan civilisation ends in the year 2012, for they could not foresee what would happen after the great awakening. The year 2012 marks the end of life as we know it. In the entire history of the planet there has never been an opportunity like this for spiritual growth. Your task is to prepare yourself and be ready to take the leap. Stop wandering round the maze of life in confusion and fear. It is time now to walk confidently and purposefully into a new arena.

In this book I am offering you a simple guide to take you from novice to top player. *A Little Light on the Spiritual Laws* will enable you to master life.

*Follow
The Spiritual Laws
and you will create
Heaven on Earth.*

AN OVERVIEW
OF THE
SPIRITUAL SCHEME

We all incarnate to experience life in a physical body. Earth is a mystery school, a place where our lessons are presented to us in the form of situations or particular people. It is the way in which we deal with our life circumstances that determines whether or not we pass our examinations. When we respond to all our tests with compassion, strength and understanding we become masters.

The aim of everyone who incarnates on Earth is ascension or enlightenment, which is the total mastery of all the lessons offered here. This may take many lifetimes for, if we hurt or harm another we earn karma, which is a debt and must be repaid. Very often our soul will want us to return to Earth to meet the same people and similar situations in order to experience the challenges again or to complete unresolved issues.

Earth is a very special learning establishment in the Universe. Here we are offered lessons about sexuality, emotions and finances, which are not available elsewhere. We also have a physical body, which is built according to our mental and emotional states.

When we are born we forget our spiritual connection and our past experiences on Earth or elsewhere. However, we do not walk our pathway alone. We all have a guardian angel who is with us throughout all our lives. Angels are pure spiritual beings from higher dimensions, who have rarely taken a physical body. Our guardian angel protects us, encourages us and is our voice of conscience. When we are ready we also attract other angels to us for a specific purpose or to work with us.

Everyone also has a spirit guide, who has lived on Earth and volunteered after death to train as a guide to help those who are still here. Your spirit guide is attracted to you according to the light you radiate, and different guides come to you as you change. An evolved person will attract greater guides. We have many guides who help us with different aspects of our lives. We also have helpers. These are usually the spirits of people who have loved us in life and want to help us after they die.

While your angels and guides look after you on a daily basis, there are many great angels who are higher up the angelic hierarchy, the Archangels, Principalities and Powers in particular, who are watching over the scheme on Earth. There are also ascended masters, those who have already mastered the lessons on Earth, and are helping the whole planet to evolve. We can ask them in prayer or meditation for help. In overall command is the Source, who is known as God, Brahma, the Creator, the Godhead or the Divine.

We can ask any of these invisible spirits for help and they will do what they can within the possibilities of the spiritual laws.

We are multi-dimensional beings. A dimension is a frequency range. This means that part of us may be stuck in low frequency negative emotions while another part is radiating compassion and love into the Universe. Simplistically, the first dimension is the mineral kingdom, where new ideas are rooted. The second dimension is the plant world, which needs light to grow. Light contains spiritual information and knowledge.

AN OVERVIEW
. . . . OF THE . . . .
SPIRITUAL SCHEME

The third dimension is the animal kingdom. Very materialistic and negative people are also in this dimensional frequency and have often forgotten their divine connections. Our planet is now moving into the fourth dimension. At this frequency humans begin to remember past lives and the truth about who they are. The heart begins to open to unconditional love.

In order to move into the frequency of the fifth dimension people must have forgiven themselves and others. Fear and negativity will have been transmuted. Here is the understanding of Oneness. The sixth dimension is the frequency which we rise to when we leave our physical bodies after ascension and are purifying our light body for greater service in the universes. The seventh dimension is known as the seventh heaven. This is where the higher ascended masters and most of the angels reside.

Your soul is a higher aspect of you, which holds all the experiences of your journeys through many planes of existence. A part of your soul, which is your personality self, has been sent to Earth to learn. While your higher self or soul knows that you are a spiritual being in a human body, your lower or personality aspect has forgotten. Your task on Earth is to remember who you are. Many people are in a soul sleep and unaware that they are spiritual beings. Their higher selves are sending difficulties and pain, which are wake up calls to set them seeking and searching for the truth.

A window of opportunity has opened now for spiritual growth. Many souls are wishing to incarnate to take advantage of it. We have the chance to pay off all our karmic debts and master our lessons. At this time there is also more spiritual guidance and help available to us than ever before

so that we can move quickly towards ascension. In order
to do so it helps to understand the spiritual laws so that
we can move forward with clarity and understanding on
our journey.

THE
BASIC LAWS
OF
LIFE

CHAPTER ONE

AS ABOVE, SO BELOW

As above so below. This is the first Law of the Universe. On Earth as it is in heaven.

If you are a parent you love all your children the same whether they are babies, toddlers or adults. You believe in them, even though they may be going through a difficult phase. A mother may shake her head in sorrow at the behaviour of her young children, but she does not judge them. She knows they will grow up.

The parents of a small child do not love him less because he is jealous of his baby sister. They understand and try to help him with his conflicting feelings. When he is older they do not stop loving him because he struggles with his homework. They offer help.

God does not stop loving you when you have turbulent emotions or find a piece of work difficult. Nor does He judge you. Rather you are encouraged and helped by His angels.

The Universe loves you and holds a vision of your future as an enlightened person no matter what mistakes you are making on Earth.

Wise parents gently direct and encourage their children to develop their talents. At the same time they give them freedom to learn from their own mistakes. The more sensible a child is the more freedom of choice you allow him.

We cannot always prevent our children from suffering the

consequences of their actions. Strong-willed children follow their own desires into trouble. Have you ever watched a toddler determined to touch the hot stove despite being told a dozen times it will hurt? Often it is only the experience of hurt that allows them to learn.

We too are given free choice. Like any sensible parent, the Divine will step in and try to guide us if we are going wildly off track. However, under spiritual law God will not force us to do His will. If we are hell-bent, He will stand back and allow us to learn the hard way.

As in any family, young souls are carefully supervised by God while evolved souls are given responsibility for themselves.

The Universe waits without judgment as we experience and learn. When we are ready it opens new doors.

Do you want those you love to be happy, fulfilled, prosperous and healthy? If you really love them of course you do. Equally Source wants you, His beloved child, to be happy, fulfilled, prosperous and healthy.

I talked to someone who felt guilty because she was so happy in her job. Somehow she felt God must disapprove of her for being so joyous about her work! The reverse is true.

When you are happy heaven rejoices. God's will is for you to do what gives you joy, fulfilment and a sense of worth.

A wise parent offers guidance to his children and empowers them to make free choices. If they ignore the guidance, the loving parent supports them in whatever they decide to do.

God too offers us guidance in dreams, meditation or through the prompting of intuition. He gives us entirely free choice about whether we accept it or not and supports us unconditionally whichever path we choose. He is not attached to us making a particular choice.

While you have free choice, your soul is longing for you to choose the path of greatest spiritual growth. However, most of us have to learn from experience that foolhardy, selfish choices lead to ill health, failure and misery.

We often find out the hard way that when we act from our lower will, which is our own selfish desire, the inevitable result is that we feel bad.

John was an old-fashioned, authoritarian figure, tall, scowling when crossed and jovial when he got his own way. His grandfather founded the family business. It passed to his father and then to him. He assumed that his son, Ronald, would take over. Ronald, however, wanted to be a musician and showed considerable talent. John, the father, was utterly intransigent. He derided his son's musical ability and did everything in his power to manipulate and emotionally blackmail him to enter the family firm. John always claimed that he was acting in his son's best interests, for no one could earn a respectable living as a musician. He said he was only trying to save Ronald from grief and disappointment.

John's controlling actions were fear based. Not surprisingly he felt permanently irritable and quarrelled with his wife as well as his son. These factors exacerbated his heart condition. Eventually Ronald decided to break away from his family completely so that he could express himself through his music. His father felt isolated, ill and insecure as a result of his own alienating actions. These were the very feelings he was trying to avoid by controlling his son.

A wise parent encourages his child to express his talent and is not attached to the child following one pathway. Fear-based choices come from our lower will. 'Let thy will be done' means, 'help me to make choices from my higher self'. Wise, courageous choices result in happiness, health and abundance.

Choices that promote love, harmony and joy come from the higher or divine will and always empower us.

We all like to be appreciated. When someone thanks us from the bottom of their heart for something we have done, we feel a sense of satisfaction and delight and often want to give more. And so it is above. The heavens smile on us when we appreciate and say thank you for what we have received. The powers of the Universe then send us more.

Many people tell me that they are screaming at their angels for help and simply cannot understand why assistance is not forthcoming. Take an example from Earth below. Your child is screaming at you to help him with his homework. Ten to one you feel exasperated and quite disinclined to satisfy him. No wonder the angels turn a deaf ear to selfish screams for help. When your child asks pleasantly and you have a sense that he is ready to value your help, you are undoubtedly delighted to give it. So too are the forces of light.

When you are ready to receive something from the Universe, ask calmly and pleasantly. They will be delighted to let you have it. Value it when you get it.

.

It is repellent to be with a negative person. If you try to help someone who prefers to wallow in misery, after a while you will probably walk away. If you care for them you may keep an eye on them from a distance. It is the same in the heavens.

The angels find it very difficult to access you through determined negativity. They can only stand by to help.

If someone is kind to you or your animals, you warm to them. When you are kind to yourself or any of God's creatures the Universe warms to you. When someone is enthusiastic you feel sparked and motivated to action. So it is with the energy of the Universe. It will support your passion. If someone has faith in you, you live up to their faith. When we have faith in God, He responds to our faith. We respond to generosity. God does likewise.

You cannot manipulate or bargain with a wise parent. You cannot manipulate or bargain with God.

The same things
 touch God's heart as touch
a human heart.

CHAPTER TWO

AS WITHIN, SO WITHOUT

Earth is a place of learning where our lessons are presented to us by making our outside world an exact reflection of our inner world.

If you are angry inside, even though you may have buried the anger so deeply you are unaware of it, you will find angry people in your life. They are mirroring your denied anger back to you.

If you have a deep sense of abandonment, which may well have originated in another life, people will reflect that back to you. They may leave you, withdraw emotionally or even die.

If you are self-critical and constantly beat yourself up with your thoughts, you will attract people who will reflect this by putting you down or even physically hitting you.

The person who feels secure, loved, safe and happy inside will have a secure, safe and happy life surrounded by people who love him or her. Your inner integrity will be matched by those around you. The people in your life will be creative, generous-hearted, honest or modest to the extent that you are.

The Universe rearranges itself to reflect your reality.
Literally as within so without.

Bob and Marguerite had ended their relationship and were in conflict. He kept telling her and everyone else that he wanted them to make peace. She was not interested. She verbally attacked him whenever she saw him. Bob was in despair. He hated fighting and simply did not know how to bring peace into the situation.

A very wise friend of his drew him aside one day and said, 'Bob. She feels threatened by you. She's not ready to make peace yet. The only way you can handle it is to find peace within yourself.'

This was such a revelation to him that when he was telling me this he cried. Spiritual law is so simple. Peace within leads to peace in your life. When everyone finds inner peace there will automatically be world peace.

This law even applies to the physical body. Inner feelings are reflected in the way we build our bodies.

If we feel emotionally or sexually vulnerable inside, we may build a protective layer of fat over our abdomen or hips, the places where we hold our emotions and sexuality.

If at an inner level we feel not really lovable, we may build a big chest to protect our heart centre. Macho men with muscly chests are often hiding feelings of vulnerability. A woman will unconsciously build big breasts to indicate her need to nurture or be nurtured.

If we feel deep inside that we must shoulder the responsibility for our family or even the world, we will build ourselves big shoulders. If, on the other hand, we have no intention or desire to carry responsibility we will build sloping shoulders that allow burdens to slip off.

Your body is a mirror of your deep, often unconscious, inner feelings.

So, if you have a pain in the neck, ask yourself, 'Who am I allowing to be a pain in the neck?' When you have re-empowered yourself you no longer need to have a pain in this location. It is also possible that you are being a pain to yourself!

The same principle applies to a pain in the backside. 'Who is a pain in the backside?'

Pain in the heart. 'Who am I allowing to hurt me?'

Indigestion. 'What experience can't I assimilate?'

An ache. 'Who or what am I aching for?'

If you cannot hear, you ask, 'What don't I want to hear?' or 'Who don't I want to listen to?'

If you have stiff hips, ask yourself, 'How can I change my attitude to moving forward?'

I knew George very well. He was a young man of great wisdom. His fault if anything was to be able to see everyone's point of view, so he was not able to push himself forward or really stand up for himself. He was involved with a very difficult business partner who kept pulling the rug from under him. The situation was going round in circles.

One day he said to me, 'My right hip is so stiff. I can't understand what it's about.'

Stiff hips reflect an inability to move forward in life. Anything on the right side of the body mirrors attitudes to do with men, the future or our career. The left side reflects our attitudes to women, the past or our home life. So George's hips were very accurately telling him that internally he was being rigid in his attitude to his male business partner and to the future of his business. We discussed what he could do to change.

Life in the amazing school of Earth gives us constant opportunities to learn about ourselves. Your animals will reflect your inner qualities back to you. What are your animals like? What qualities do they have?

WITHOUT

When we laughingly say that someone is just like his dog, little do we realise it is not by chance. If your animals have seemingly different characteristics, each one is representing a part of your personality. That is why it has come into your life.

The person who appears to be very pleasant and calm, yet has an animal which is aggressive and nasty, is not expressing his underlying angry feelings. If someone appears to be flaky and messy yet has a beautiful magnificent animal, he is not in touch with the magnificence of his being.

The Law is simple and exact.

Inanimate objects too represent an aspect of their owners. When someone drives a battered, dirty old banger, the car reflects their current inner state. A smart, shiny, clean car is the outward manifestation of inner worth. A family car represents the underlying collective family feeling.

The Higher Beings who have you in their charge cause the material objects in your life to alter according to your inner state. Leaky taps, roofs, radiators in your external life reveal leaky emotions within, while raging fires outside reflect burning issues within.

Our leaders reflect the collective inner feelings of the country we live in. The teachers in our schools reflect our collective inner beliefs about the worth of our children. Prison systems, parliaments, all aspects of society directly mirror the deepest feelings of the collective consciousness of the people.

When we, who have signed up for this course on Earth, wish to change something in our lives, we must look within to alter our beliefs and attitudes in order for our outer world to change. If we wish to change society, enough people must change themselves.

This is discussed more fully in the Law of Reflection.

The Universe rearranges itself to bring you what you believe.

CHAPTER THREE

THE LAW OF REQUEST

Under spiritual law, if you want help, you must ask for it.

If you rush in and interfere in a friend's concerns in an attempt to help him, it is a quick way to lose his friendship.

Furthermore, when you help someone who has not asked for it, you prevent him from sorting out his situation for himself, which is his learning process. Quite likely you become an enabler, who helps him to continue in his old unhelpful ways. When you force your help or advice on to someone, you bear the karma if it goes wrong. It is considered bad manners to rush in uninvited and most likely your help will be ignored or unappreciated.

Of course, if someone is drowning, you help. You guide the blind person round the hole in the pavement. You comfort the sick and bereaved. However, if you feel upset by the mess someone has got themselves into, it is *your* stuff. It is an indication that you need to look at yourself rather than rescue someone else.

I am constantly being asked questions like, 'What can I do for my aunt? Since her husband died she has been so miserable and I keep trying to persuade her to meet new people but she won't.'

The answer is: When she is ready she will ask you to help her. Until that time look within at the part of you that wants to meet new people or the rejection you feel when she does not accept your help.

'I am desperate for my daughter. She refuses to marry

her boyfriend and I'm afraid she'll never get married. How can I help?'

The answer is: When your daughter has looked at her own fears she will be ready. Perhaps she knows at some deep inner level that this is not the right man for her. Maybe she knows it upsets you and this is her way of punishing you. She could have a million reasons. However, she is clearly serving you by bringing up some of your stuff. Unless she asks you for help, quit trying to help her and look at what it means to you.

If you are involved in a difficult situation at work, the learning and the experience you gain from dealing with it may be the perfect stepping stone you need to move you on in your career. It prepares you for promotion. You would not expect someone to leap in and take over the situation without asking permission. That would be interfering and block you from being ready for a better job.

In the spiritual realms no angel or Higher Being of Light would dream of interfering in your life. Yes, they will save you from serious accident if that is not your karma, or death if it is not your time.

However, they will stand by with total compassion and patience and watch you making a mess of your situation if that is what you need for your growth. Not only is it spiritual bad manners for them to interfere but it also stops you from becoming stronger and learning.

There are times when it is appropriate to ask for help. By asking, I do not mean screaming with frustration like a toddler or crying like a victim who does not want to take any responsibility for their actions. By asking, I mean carefully assessing the situation and then calmly and with strength requesting the help you need.

As soon as you are ready to ask for help you are ready to
receive it. You are ready to accept the wisdom that goes with
it. Then the higher powers will align themselves to help you.

Some people are constantly crying out, 'When, what, how, who, where?' They want to know the answer to one question after another. These are demands rather than questions. They come from a place of desperation and neediness, not from a centred open place. The person who is steadfastly walking the spiritual path goes within to look for answers. As soon as you are ready to know something more the teacher will appear to provide it. This may be in the form of a book, a person or a programme on television. When you are ready to formulate the question you are ready to know the answer.

You really do not expect to invite a solicitor to dinner, have him ask you about your will and then end up rewriting it for you over coffee. Nor does your neighbour, who is a painter and decorator, call in and uninvited touch up the paintwork in your home. This is as much interference as the healer who insists on lifting your headache or giving you healing. You may be grateful for any of these services but it contravenes spiritual law unless you ask.

If someone offers help and you accept it that is a contract. If they offer and offer and offer until you accept that is pressure. It is their stuff.

When you need help from the angels, Jesus, the ascended masters or any of the spiritual hierarchy of light, first quieten and centre yourself. Meditate on what you really want and find clarity about it. Then ask the beings to whom you wish to address your request for the help you require. They will always help you.

[15]

My daughter was feeling exhausted as she was driving to work. She thought, 'How can I energise myself for the day ahead?' No sooner had she formulated the thought than a car passed her. The letters of the number plate were AUM. She knew that she was being given an answer. Aum, om or ohm is the sacred sound of the Universe and is a very powerful mantra. She sounded the Aum all the way to work and felt much better.

Remember the answer lies in the question. The more clarity you have in your question, the fuller the help you will receive.

The Universe is waiting to help you. All you have to do is ask.

CHAPTER FOUR

THE LAW OF ATTRACTION

I remember playing with magnets as a child and being fascinated by the way some objects were attracted to them and others jumped away. Even more things appeared to be inert and indifferent to the magnets. I did not understand the laws of physics but I thought it was great fun.

If you had magnets stuck all over you, you would expect some things to stick to you, others to leap away and still more to show no reaction. In a sense this is what happens in life. You unconsciously transmit your energy. Some of your qualities are magnetic and others repellent. You have drawn towards you everything and everyone who is in your life. Other things and people you have repelled. Many situations have no magnetic pull towards you. For example, you may not attract a condition of starvation or homelessness because you do not send out the vibration which brings it to you.

A radio transmitter broadcasts on a particular frequency. Anyone interested in a programme going out on that waveband tunes in. You are a transmitter. You broadcast the play of your life. You send out into the ether the story of your patterns, emotional energy, mindsets, denials, likes and dislikes and much more.

Imagine you want to find an interesting programme. There are hundreds to tune into and you are flicking through the channels trying to decide which one to listen to. Most of them you tune out immediately. Now and again one will catch your attention. It may be heavy or funny, boring or interesting, violent or peaceful. Something about it draws you to stay tuned in. You may like some aspects but be repelled by others. Nevertheless you are hooked in.

In the same way we attract people to us. People who do not resonate on our frequency simply are not attracted to us. They pass on by.

The vibration you emit is made up of your conscious and unconscious energy, some repellent, some magnetic, some neutral. The underlying law is *like attracts like*. We attract into our lives people and situations that have similar vibrations to our own.

Negative qualities such as neediness, desperation, depression, greed, unkindness or thoughtlessness transmit on a low frequency. If we have elements of these in our nature, we will magnetise someone with similar energy into our life. Qualities such as love, kindness, happiness, delight or generosity transmit a high-frequency energy and also magnetise people with similar energy.

I hear people say, 'I can't understand why he is in my life. He is so negative and nothing like I am.' Or, 'Why did that person cheat me? I am so honest.'

Spiritual law is exact. The Universe provides mirrors for us to look into. Look around you and note the characters around you. They are taking part in the play of your life for a reason. The more vehemently we deny that we are magnets for a particular type of person or situation, the more our Higher Self is asking us to look at our shadow. This is a negative aspect of ourselves that we deny.

If you feel ready to commit to a relationship but your partner will not do so, look within at your own fear of commitment. He or she simply would not be there if you were one hundred percent sure. The moment you resolve your underlying belief, the other person will either commit to you or leave your life and allow someone who can commit to enter. The person who is always cheerful and happy but seems to be surrounded by depressed people has attracted them to mirror their inner unhappiness. They serve a purpose, possibly to make them feel needed.

Desperation repels. A couple I knew were absolutely desperate to have a baby. They had tried everything. They went everywhere. There was no physical reason why they could not conceive a baby. Psychics kept telling them that a soul was waiting to enter but their desperation repelled an incoming soul. They decided to surrender and make their lives fulfilling without a child. As soon as they did this an energy shift took place. They sent out a magnetic energy of contentment, which drew in a spirit from the Universe, and suddenly they were expecting a baby. A similar thing often happens when someone is desperate for a partner. People pick up the desperation on a subtle level and move away. When they change that energy into a loving, accepting, open energy the right person is attracted in.

Our underlying beliefs attract situations and people to us. If you have a belief that you are not deserving, you will attract people into your life who mirror that belief back to you by treating you badly.

If you believe that you have to serve others, you attract people who need to be looked after in some way.

If you have a belief that no one could possibly understand you, you will magnetise people who do not understand you.

A woman who constantly attracted partners who deceived her realised that she had an underlying belief that it is not

safe to trust, which allowed her to draw in people capable
of deception. When she healed this belief, she attracted a
trustworthy partner.

A woman called Jane reminded me of an emerald-green
swamp. She was beautiful on the surface but if you stepped
too close you got sucked into the ooze. She was bubbly and
jolly as an acquaintance but in close personal relationships
she became demanding, needy, jealous and a drama queen. Of
course, unconsciously she broadcast her advertisement for an
actor who would take part in this particular play. She attracted
men who were ripe to be deceived by the outer appearance. She
complained about the type of men in her life. They moaned
about her. However, they were inevitably magnetised towards
each other's energies and would continue to be so until they
changed their vibration.

If a man broadcasts, 'I am controlling and I am looking
for a woman who I can dominate,' he will attract women who
will allow themselves to be dominated. It will almost certainly
be unconscious. An empowered woman would not be drawn
to this vibration. The person who keeps drawing the same
type of person into their lives is continuing to broadcast the
same message.

The Law of Attraction works on many levels. If you are
out of harmony with life you may attract food which disagrees
with you. If you think self-critical thoughts you are taking
little swipes at yourself. You may attract mosquitoes which
bite you. They are serving as a reflection of the energy you are
sending out. If you are burying rage you may draw in attack.
These things may, of course, be a return of karma, which is
the inevitable balancing of right and wrong over lifetimes.

Whenever you do something because you feel you should

or ought to, then you are in bondage. You will attract situations and people that keep you in bondage. If, on the other hand, you are sending out positive energy, you will attract help when you need it. A friend told me how she was lost, completely lost, in the country. She saw an animal in the field in front of her and wasn't sure whether it was a bull or a cow. As she looked doubtfully at it, a woman appeared from nowhere and without preamble said, 'It's OK, that's a cow. You are lost. I will show you the way.' She led her past the animal on to the correct path. My friend had attracted the help she needed at that moment.

If you think negative thoughts you attract negative situations and people. If you have ill health, the moment you are ready to let it go you will attract the perfect healer into your life. If you want a project to succeed but you have underlying feelings of boredom or you are scared or tired, the underlying energy will counteract the success of the project. Whenever something is not materialising as you expect, examine your underlying feelings and change them. Then magnetise what you do want.

The inner attracts the outer. If something in your outer world is not what you want it to be, look inside and shift how you feel about yourself. You will then automatically attract different people and experiences to you.

If, for instance, you want a committed partner look at how you commit to loving yourself. The moment you truly commit to loving yourself the external will change and you will attract someone committed to loving you.

If you put yourself down and never think you are good

enough, you will attract an abuser who will do the same to you. Remind yourself of your good qualities and magnetise someone who appreciates you.

What about the highly evolved spiritual person who works with drug addicts or violent criminals? This happens where they have made a pre-life agreement to work with these people. It may also be a karmic consequence of something unresolved from another lifetime.

And, of course, there are cases where opposite poles attract. Someone radiating light may draw dark vibrations towards them but will not be affected by them. A dark place such as a prison may draw enlightened people who wish to take the light in.

Do not send out negative energy and wait for a disaster to be magnetised towards you. Send out positive light and wait for a miracle to be drawn towards you.

 You are a magnet: you attract like to you.

CHAPTER FIVE

THE LAW OF RESISTANCE

I was watching two children at play. The little girl had set out a tea party in the garden playhouse. She called her brother to come in for tea but when he arrived at the door she pushed it closed on him and would not let him in. A struggle ensued and the little girl became angry and tired as she tried to prevent her brother from entering.

We may laugh at children and say how silly they can be. However, we often do similar things in life.

Every time we focus on something we are calling it towards us. With our thoughts and beliefs, we invite people, situations and material things into our life. When they arrive, if we do not really want them, we try to push them away again.

I was chatting to a neighbour who told me she was sure her mother-in-law was going to stay with them for Christmas and ruin it for everyone. She said, 'I can just see it all. It's a nightmare.' Of course, her strong pictures and fears were inevitably drawing her mother-in-law in, while her anger was shutting the door on her. My neighbour was using her vital energy in resistance.

Many people invoke the Law of Resistance without being aware of what they are doing. Your unconscious mind and the universal mind work exactly like computers. You cannot tell a computer *not* to bring up a certain file for it cannot accept negative instructions. It will assume you *do* want that file and bring it up.

Your conscious mind can discriminate between a negative instruction and a positive one but your unconscious mind cannot tell the difference. If your conscious mind is fully engaged on driving, watching TV or concentrating very hard on something, your unconscious mind may receive the message. For example, when a child is concentrating on his homework his conscious mind is fully occupied. If at that moment his mother says, 'Don't you dare get it wrong,' his unconscious mind takes the comment. It ignores the 'don't' and receives a message to 'get it wrong'. It is far better to say positively, 'You can get it right.' Similarly, if a man's mind is completely absorbed on the lecture he is preparing and his wife says, 'Don't be late for the dinner party,' she is setting up a problem ahead. It would be preferable to say, 'Remember the dinner party starts at 8 o'clock.'

If you think a thought or make a statement often enough, it will access your unconscious mind. Some people have illness in their lives because they resist illness. If you are continuously thinking 'I don't want to be ill', the word 'ill' filters constantly into your unconscious mind. Your computer looks for a programme which will make you ill.

Your unconscious mind is also open when you are relaxed. When you are relaxing in the sunshine it is a bad time to worry, for you may manifest your fears. It is an excellent time to picture what you want to create in your life.

'Don't', 'can't', 'won't' or 'not' are words which invoke the Law of Resistance.

The thought 'I won't ever find a perfect partner' resists the perfect partner.

THE LAW
OF
RESISTANCE

'I don't want to be poor' brings you poverty.

'I can't live in that awful house' keeps you living in that awful house.

'I'm not a difficult person', if repeated enough, brings out your difficult personality.

'I won't ever be like my mother' ensures you become just like her.

You become what you resist. Whatever you resist persists in your life and uses up your energy in struggle.

'I am healthy' is a command that goes into the computer and is magnetic to health.

'I deserve a perfect partner' attracts a perfect partner.

'I welcome riches' draws riches into your life.

'I live in a beautiful home' brings a beautiful home to you.

The affirmation 'I am wise' starts to put you in touch with your wisdom.

Never resist failure or poverty. Instead attract success and wealth. Always embrace the positive rather than resisting the negative.

I holidayed in a community where they decided to take the structure out of work groups. Instead they asked people to volunteer to help. The result was that everyone felt freer and had more time to relax. They realised that the structured rules put pressure on people and resulted in resistance, which took energy.

Releasing control frees energy.

A young man came to speak to me after a talk I gave on abundance. He said that a switch had gone on in his head – click – as he listened. Up to that time he had felt he was not deserving. He realised he had been resisting anything beyond his level of deservingness. I saw him a few weeks later at an Angel workshop and he told me that he had stopped resisting and started to embrace what he really wanted in life. This shift in attitude had transformed his prosperity levels.

Sometimes change takes a little longer than this. If you have been resisting loneliness for a long time, there will be a huge thought-form of loneliness around you. You may have been using all your energy to hold this fear back, so it could take a little time to transmute it. One positive way of dissolving a thought-form you have been resisting is to write down and then burn all your fears about it. Then write down what you do want and start to attract what you want. You will find you have more energy.

If two people want to push a boulder in a certain direction, they will both stand on the same side of the boulder and push so that it moves. If, however, they stand opposite each other and push, it will move only to the extent that one is stronger. This is what our inner personalities do when they struggle. If we have two personalities within us working for the same end our life flows smoothly forward. If we have two inner personalities working in resistance to one another, we stay stuck. For example, if part of us is afraid of commitment and another part of us wants a close and stable relationship, then we will create a pull-push situation. The relationship will stay stuck and we will wonder why we feel so tired.

If you are working with someone on a project and you both have the same vision, the project inevitably moves forward. However, if you are in conflict, the resistance will result in delays. That person is not in your life by chance. He or she is mirroring back to you your own doubts, fears or disquiet.

Look within and decide what you truly want and what your vision really is. When you resolve your inner conflict, the other person must, under universal law, leave your life or change their attitude.

The Law of Resistance is triggered by victim consciousness. A victim is someone who blames others for their fate, believes the world owes them a living and that they cannot possibly look after themselves. When someone is thinking, 'Poor me. I can't look after myself,' or 'I am so unlucky,' he is being a victim who is resisting the abundance, generosity and caring of the Divine. If someone is blaming another for what is happening in his own life, he is a victim who is resisting taking personal responsibility for what he has created.

A very bitter lady called Andrea said to me of her husband, 'The awful situation in our marriage is totally due to him. He goes out every night and makes me so angry.' She was resisting taking responsibility for her attitude which caused him to go out every night. She was resisting his good qualities. She told me he didn't have any. Andrea painted a picture of herself as an angry saint.

It was only when she stopped resisting and started to take an honest look at her own actions that she became calmer. Her husband stayed in a couple of evenings and she focused on the good qualities in him that she had discovered. They had a pleasant time. When she no longer blamed him, stopped resisting him going out and embraced him staying at home, their marriage improved unbelievably.

When we feel angry or guilty we resist the joy of life and the magnificence of self.

Most of us have at some time resisted doing a job of work. We resist the ironing until the pile is enormous or doing the garden until it is overgrown or that report that needs to be written until it assumes horrendous proportions. Any task appears difficult in direct proportion to our level of resistance.

Anything that you are resisting has a message for you. For instance, if you are resisting poverty, it is time to look at what poverty is trying to say to you. Are you afraid of lack? What exactly do you fear? Open up to what you do want, not what you don't want.

So, if you are made redundant it is not by chance. You have activated the laws of the Universe to take your job away. You have created redundancy in your life for a purpose, so examine the underlying reason and learn from it. Did you feel dissatisfied or grumble about your work? The Universe received the message that you did not want that job. If you felt undervalued, affirm your value. If you did not trust your boss, build up your trust levels.

If you have a recurring pattern of failure constantly picture yourself succeeding.

Quit resisting. Decide what you do want in life and start to send out magnetic, excited, enthusiastic energies to draw the positive to you.

*What you resist persists
in your life and drains you
of energy. Embrace what
you do want and feel alive.*

CHAPTER SIX

THE LAW OF REFLECTION

Earth is an amazing place of learning where you are constantly being given an opportunity to look at yourself in a mirror. The mirror of the Universe is so honest and accurate that your deepest secrets show up in the reflections you see of yourself. Every single person and situation in your life is a mirror of an aspect of you. As within so without.

When you see yourself in a mirror you may not like what you see, you may claim the reflection is distorted but you rarely insist that it is someone else entirely that you see. When the Universe presents us with someone or something in life this is equally a mirror. We can rant about it or deny it. However, the spiritual Law of Reflection reminds us to look in the mirror and change ourselves.

When you look in a mirror and see that your eyes look heavy and tired, you do not try to change the reflection. You eat a healthier diet and get more sleep so that the reflection changes.

When there is someone in your life who you do not like you can, of course, spend time and energy trying to fix or change him or her. If you do this you are trying to change the reflection. It is a form of denial. People who do this are known as rescuers. They would rather spend time changing the reflection than working on themselves. When you understand the Law of Reflection you never again try to get someone else to be different in order that you feel more comfortable. You observe the outer and change the inner.

REFLECTION

Those people in your life that you do not like are showing you aspects of yourself you do not feel comfortable with. If you have a friend who seems very callous, ask yourself where you are hard-hearted. If your child is hostile, look within at your own anger. Imagine that your boss is completely disorganised and chaotic. If you pride yourself on your togetherness and your sense of responsibility, you are probably quite angry at him for being so unlike you and may well tell yourself he is not a mirror.

Nevertheless, look within yourself for an aspect of you that is untidy. Possibly a little bit of you wants to be carefree and irresponsible. If as a child you were kept under tight discipline or there were high expectations of you, there may be a part of you that is fearful of making a mistake or being careless. If you have always had to be responsible and in control, it is terrifying to let go. The inner part of you that wants to be irresponsible is reflected in people around you. To the extent that you are angry at your boss, you are angry at the chaotic part of yourself that appears in the mirror.

If someone in your life has an attribute which genuinely does not bother you, it does not reflect you and you will not even notice it.

The more a characteristic in someone else bothers you,
the more your soul is trying to draw a reflection to
your attention.

All the people that you really like are mirroring aspects of yourself that you feel good about. Take anyone that you like, respect or admire. Think about the qualities that you like about them. Those qualities are to some extent within you. You would not have attracted that person, nor would you notice those parts of them, if they were not within you. The magic mirror of the Universe is showing you a beautiful part of yourself that you may not be in touch with. Enhance these qualities by practising them and more people with these fine characteristics will enter your life.

If the Universe really wants to draw your attention to something it will give you three mirrors to look into at once.

A client said to me, 'I've seen three birds with broken wings this week. What does that tell me?'

You cannot fly with a broken wing. I suggested she looked at where she felt her freedom was curtailed. Immediately she said that her husband did not want her to go to workshops as she was spending too much time away from him. She felt really restricted. The Universe was mirroring back to her the sense of her wings being clipped. It was time for her to communicate honestly with her husband.

If you notice three blind people one day it might suggest you are not seeing something. If you notice three accidents you might consider where you are going too fast or heading for disaster.

Everything is a reflection.

Water reflects what is happening to your emotions or spirituality. If your emotions are leaking, in other words you have unshed emotions, you may find taps drip, radiators leak. I knew someone whose roof leaked and the water dripped on to his divorce papers. Nothing else was touched, only these papers. He had never really dealt with the feelings about the break-up of his marriage. Rivers, lakes, oceans carry the emotional and spiritual life-force of an area. Are you drawn to turbulent seas or tranquil lakes? Remember too that water symbolically washes and purifies.

Fire is hot and bright. A camp fire or a fire in the hearth may indicate a peaceful centre. A rampaging out-of-control conflagration reflects the anger and hostility of all those affected by it. Fire is also a great transmuter of negative energy.

Earth is solid but can be suffocating or boring. If you get stuck in the mud, it has something to tell you about your life. An earthquake tells you that foundations of your life you thought were secure are not. From earth there is new growth.

Air has great energy. It represents communication and new ideas. If you are sitting in a draught which irritates you it may be that someone's communication is irritating you. A hurricane is blowing away outmoded thinking from an area and heralding the new. Fresh air also blows away cobwebs.

Every part of your car represents some aspect of you. If your brakes fail it may be warning you to stop something you are doing.

The lights do not work. Can you see where you are going in life?

The paintwork gets scratched or battered. Are you feeling dented or battered? Maybe you are being critical of self.

The horn refuses to make a sound. Is it time to speak up for yourself? You have a puncture. Are you feeling deflated? Is someone letting you down? How are you letting yourself down or not supporting yourself?

Flat battery. Are you feeling flat? Have you run out of energy?

If you cannot work out what the reflection is, talk about what that piece of the machine does. For instance, my car keys have batteries in them. The battery went dead on the spare one. Before I had time to deal with it, the other went flat. Neither worked and I could not get into my car. The spare key allows other people access to my car (me). My key allows me access (to my consciousness). The battery is the energy which fuels them. As they had both run out they were reflecting to me that I was too tired to give anything to anyone else or myself.

Gears facilitate the movement from one speed to another. If they are grating, are you having difficulty making a move in your life or simply in shifting your consciousness about something?

Animals reflect the qualities and characteristics of their owners. A well-disciplined, good-natured, friendly dog reflects an owner you can trust and feel comfortable with. A wild, savage, noisy animal will warn you to be careful of its owner even if the surface impression is of a gentle person. We are complex people and the different animals we own will reflect different aspects of us. Your cat may reflect your coolly detached work mode, while your dog shows your exuberant, friendly home personality.

Ask someone what his or her animal is like and you will learn about them.

As I was writing this chapter, with synchronicity, I read an article about the qualities and attitudes of different dogs. We choose a dog consciously or unconsciously to match ourselves.

Steady, solid, tolerant and good-natured breeds include Basset hound, bloodhound, beagle, bulldog, Saint Bernard, mastiff, Irish wolfhound and Newfoundland.

Clever dogs who are trainable and observant are Doberman, Cardigan Welsh Corgi, Shetland sheepdog and poodle.

Protective dogs who are territorial and dominant include boxer, Rottweiler, bull terrier, chow chow, bullmastiff, and giant schnauzer.

Friendly, affectionate dogs are border terrier, bearded collie, English setter, English springer spaniel, golden retriever, old English sheepdog, labrador, Cavalier King Charles Spaniel and cocker spaniel.

Independent, strong-willed animals include Afghan hound, Airedale terrier, Dalmatian, greyhound, Irish setter, pointer and foxhound.

Self-assured, spontaneous and often audacious dogs include Jack Russell terrier, miniature pinscher, West Highland white terrier, Yorkshire terrier and Irish terrier.

Consistent, self-contained and home-loving dogs are chihuahua, dachshund, King Charles spaniel, pug, Pekingese, whippet, Boston terrier and Maltese.

All animals, plants, trees and even crystals represent qualities. The oak tree in your garden reflects your solid, dependable aspect. Because of the fear and loathing held in the collective mind about insects, they often mirror our shadow side. If your garden is flamboyant and colourful it externalises an extrovert part of you, whether you consciously show it or not. If it is very neat and ordered and tidy you are likely to be the same. A family garden will reflect the predominant family characteristics.

Whatever comes into your life, look into the mirror and see what it has to teach you. Once we understand the Law of Reflection we can expand our spiritual growth by looking at what life is telling us. Our journey on Earth becomes a fascinating and exciting experience.

There are two ways to interpret what you see in a mirror.

One is that you are seeing your projection. The other that you are seeing an aspect that you have attracted. To find a projection, talk about the person or situation. For example you may say, 'You are a generous but aggravating person.' Look within at your generous aspect and the part of you that is aggravating.

To find how you attracted the reflection, be aware of how the person or situation makes you feel. For example, 'You make me feel inadequate' shows you a reflection of your inadequacy.

For further information see the chapters on The Laws of Projection and The Law of Attraction.

Never try to change someone else for they are reflecting you. So look within and change yourself.

CHAPTER SEVEN

THE LAW OF PROJECTION

On Earth aspects of self are reflected back to us. All that we perceive outside self is a mirror of something within. Therefore everything that we see outside ourselves is a projection. We take an aspect of self, for instance stubbornness, and imagine that quality is in those around us.

We project our stuff, both good and bad, on to other people and assume it is within them, often denying it is within us.

The truth is this:

You can only see yourself

You can only hear yourself

You can only talk to yourself

You can only criticise yourself

You can only praise yourself

Every time you say the words 'You are' or 'he is' or 'she is' you are projecting something of yourself on to someone else. It way be 'You are weird', in which case you unconsciously see some of your own weirdness within that person. When you say 'she is stupid', you are projecting your stupidity on to her. Or it may be 'You are wonderful', because you see something of your own wonder within them. If you tell others they are wise but do not accept your own wisdom, you are projecting your wisdom externally.

When we assume that someone else feels as we do, it is a projection. 'You must feel awful about that' or 'You must feel so delighted' are both projections. You are putting your feelings on to the other person. They may feel completely different. 'No one likes rice pudding' is a projection. So is 'Of course she likes horses' said of someone you do not know.

Jill was unhappily married whereas Kate loved her husband and had a really supportive relationship. Jill often said to Kate, 'You ought to leave your husband.' She was projecting on to her friend the part of herself that felt she ought to leave her marriage.

We project our fears on to the world. I heard someone say to her partner, 'You are a mouse. You don't have the guts to stand up for yourself.' It may be perfectly true that he does not have the guts. Nevertheless, she would not perceive this unless some part of her was afraid to stand up for herself. Although she was a big macho woman, she was projecting a timid part of herself on to him.

'You have no sense of humour' merely means that the other person does not see things in the same way as you do. They may have a fabulous but different sense of humour. You are actually commenting on yourself.

It is more comfortable to imagine that someone else has the qualities we wish to deny are within ourselves.

If you bury your hostility and express it as passive anger you will project hostility on to those around you and will imagine people are aggressive whether they are or not. You will selectively imagine angry or threatening attitudes where none are intended or expressed. Those who project their hatred think everyone is out to get them.

A young lady complained to me that her partner kept saying to her, 'You don't know how to love.' When I explained about projections she clearly recognised that her partner was talking about part of himself. It may or may not have had anything to do with her. However, we explored why she had attracted that comment. She realised that there was a grain of truth in it and started to look at the way she closed down her heart.

We project our insecurities and our sexuality on to others. The person who is paranoid about the morality of others is projecting their own underlying immorality.

The boss who suspects all his employees are cheating him is projecting his inner cheat. As a consequence of this he may well attract cheats.

The wife who constantly accuses her faithful husband of infidelity is projecting her own lack of faith in the relationship.

If you hear someone saying of another, 'She is an obdurate woman,' wonder about the obduracy of the person saying it. Someone without that quality does not need to say this of another.

Because many of us do not own or believe in our magnificence, we also project our beautiful, gracious, powerful and brilliant parts on to others. Every time you think good things about people, remember that there is something of that quality within you. Otherwise you would not have seen it within them.

We project our love on to others. Also our kindness, our generosity, our goodness. The person who is innately kind will imagine that all around her are also kind.

The deeply generous person expects others to be so.

When a couple is in love, each is projecting their inner beauty on to the other. Seeing our radiance magnified and reflected in another offers a great opportunity for spiritual growth. Being in love is a state of grace.

Generalised projections are very common, such as 'Everyone is afraid of tigers'. 'All women are chatterboxes'. 'Kids are such hard work'. Translate these projections as 'I am afraid of tigers', 'A part of myself is a chatterbox or would like to chatter' and 'I find my kids hard work'. Just take responsibility for any part that belongs to you.

Projecting yourself on to someone else prevents you from taking responsibility for self. Most people do not even realise that what they are saying is actually within them. It is a powerful form of denial.

Projection can create a game of ping-pong. When two people are shouting at each other, each accusing the other of being in the wrong, both are projecting their own anger and fear.

The expression 'a pot calling the kettle black' aptly describes the Law of Projection. Neither sees itself as black. Instead each sees how black the other is.

You can only talk to yourself. When a parent says 'You are a difficult boy' to their child, they are projecting themselves on to their offspring. This can really damage a child, who has no understanding of the reality, which is that it has nothing to do with him and everything to do with the parent. A mother who loves her baby and keeps telling him how beautiful and lovely he is, is positively projecting her open heart. She lights both up in the process.

Here are examples of projections,

'You are such a nosy person.'

'I feel you are being nosy.'

'It is difficult being a soldier.'

'The world is a terrible place.'

When we stop projecting and instead take responsibility

for our own feelings, we may say, 'I feel uncomfortable when you ask these questions,' or 'This is my business.' You say, 'I would find being a soldier very difficult,' or 'I feel very threatened by what is happening in the world.'

Even highly experienced and objective professionals of every kind see situations through coloured lenses. It is almost inevitable while we have human consciousness. When we are one hundred percent detached and able to observe from a totally objective position we can see clearly into a person or situation. Until that moment it is preferable to cut the projections out of our life.

Your life is what you experience. Other people probably experience it very differently. So watch your projections and work on yourself. Understanding this law offers enormous opportunities for personal and spiritual growth.

You do not know how anyone feels or is. Everything you see in another is a projection of an aspect of yourself.

CHAPTER EIGHT

THE LAW OF ATTACHMENT

You can have anything you wish in your life but if your sense of self-worth or your happiness *depends* on having it, then you are attached to it. Whoever or whatever you are attached to can manipulate you. You are no longer free. You are a puppet on a string.

The Universe is a soup of energy. Everything swirls and moves. Like attracts like. Certain energies repel. The dance goes on between the atoms. However, there are certain people in this great cauldron of energy that are corded together. They are drawn together from great distances and from lifetime to lifetime. The cord may bind and trap them. They will pull and tug at each other, mentally, emotionally and physically and are often completely unaware of the effect they have on each other.

Cords are formed between people who have unresolved issues between them. Every time you send thoughts or words of anger, hurt, jealousy, envy or need to someone, you manifest a tiny thread which attaches to them. An occasional thought will dissolve but if you consistently send negative feelings out, the threads will form cords or ropes. These will remain and bind you together until they are released.

In subsequent lifetimes the cords will reactivate and draw you inevitably towards those with whom you have unresolved issues. This is in order to offer your souls the opportunity to do things differently. We can also be attached to things. Negative energies such as greed, pride, need and envy can send huge cords to objects like houses, cars, jobs or bank accounts. This is why we refer to the trappings of wealth.

Cords can attach people to intangible things, for example a need for love. If you are tied to a desire for recognition this can be the psychic equivalent of having a ball and chain round your ankle. You may be corded to imprisoning energies such as self-deprecation or aloofness.

A master is detached. He is independent of status, finance or emotional need. He is free and immensely powerful.

You can have a beautiful home. Of course, God wants you to have a beautiful home. However, if you need to live in that beautiful home to give you status or security, it becomes a trapping. Cords tie you to your home and you are emotionally bound until you change your attitude. A master can enjoy a fabulous home but if it is taken away it does not affect how he feels about himself.

You can enjoy a wonderful relationship. The Source of All wants you to be happy in love. Neediness, however, cords you to your partner with the result that you are tugged to and fro emotionally. Codependent relationships enmesh you in cords so that it is difficult to feel objective about the relationship or to leave your partner.

When parents become bound to their children, it is hard to release them to adulthood. Equally a child may be so attached to a parent that it is very difficult to form a mature adult relationship with a partner.

Attachment is conditional love. A master loves unconditionally, and this does not form cords. He allows the people he loves to be free and to be themselves. If someone he loves leaves or dies, he mourns but is not devastated. He remains centred.

If you need someone to behave in a certain way in order to love them, it is not love. It is attachment. The bindings of attachment can be released in a number of ways. Love dissolves them and sets them free. You set yourself free too. When we put our hopes and expectations on people they react from their own patterns. When we accept them as they are they reveal their magnificence to us. That is love.

Forgiveness dissolves cords for all time. We are approaching the end of an era as we wait for the new higher consciousness to prevail on the planet. This means that we are now gathering in all the cords we have formed throughout our lives. Our souls now wish us to face and release all our unresolved issues and lessons so that we are free to move on. When you forgive someone and let go totally of what has happened in the past, you free that person and yourself.

Shame and guilt bind you to certain memories and hold you back. When you are ready to forgive yourself for your past actions, you dissolve these restricting cords and the memory loses its charge.

We hold on to others for our sake not theirs. Caroline told me that she wanted to spend Christmas with her partner's family but she knew her mother would be dreadfully upset. Her mother needed her, she said. At last she plucked up courage to tell her mother that she wanted to go away for Christmas. She imagined her mother withering and collapsing. Nothing of the sort. The elderly lady went out and booked herself a Christmas cruise and spent the next few weeks joyously buying new clothes. Caroline freed her mother to experience a new life.

It is very common for a whole family to be entangled in cords of codependency. It is time to pull yourself free. When you pull out your cord you may find that it is the thread that allows the whole tangle to be freed. If it is not, the family collusion is no longer your responsibility. Those involved still need to work through their part in the experience.

The other most powerful way of releasing attachment is by intention and visualisation.

John and Jean had been stuck in a codependent marriage for years. Each grumbled and complained about the other. Both were hostile. They said they wanted to separate but never quite had the courage.

John came to a workshop during which we released attachments. He set his intention to free himself and Jean. During the visualisation he brought up a clear picture of himself and his wife entangled in barbed rope. He asked for angelic help to dissolve all this and saw all the rope being cut away. Afterwards he felt a wonderful sense of release and freedom.

When he went home an interesting thing happened. Because he was detached he started seeing Jean differently. Without the negative energy constantly battering him, he remembered her sense of humour, her enthusiasm and her goodness. He started to fall in love with her all over again but this time in a mature way. Their relationship changed totally.

In this case uncording brought John and Jean together. In other cases people find that they are released to leave a relationship completely.

Detachment is a prerequisite for enlightenment

*If you wish to be free,
detach yourself from*
*everyone and everything.
It is a prerequisite for
enlightenment.*

THE
LAWS OF
CREATION

CHAPTER NINE

THE LAW OF ATTENTION

Whatever you give attention to manifests. It does not matter if it is big, small, good or bad. Spiritual Law ensures that an outcome manifests to the exact percentage you give it attention.

Attention is the focus of your thoughts, words and actions. In the material, third-dimensional world there is an expression 'seeing is believing'. However, sages have always told us 'believing is seeing'. Subatomic physics is now proving what these sages and mystics have been telling us throughout the ages. The thoughts of the experimenter affect the results of the experiment. Physicists tell us that quarks are subatomic particles formed by concentrated thought. These can now be filmed. When the individual no longer concentrates then the particles disappear. Results differ according to the expectation of the experimenter.

Lives differ according to the expectations of the individual. If ten people are in similar situations each will hold a different picture of an outcome. Accordingly each will create a slightly different result. You create your own reality. Science is now supporting this spiritual truth.

I saw this played out recently when two people I know were each putting on an event. Rebecca was organising quite a small event. She kept saying, 'There are an awful lot of seats to fill. I hope I can sell all the tickets. The cost of the advertising is too much.' These thoughts diverted her attention from the outcome she hoped for. On the night, the hall was half full.

Jane was organising quite a big show. She was clear and positive. She talked about it enthusiastically. Her attention never wavered from her vision of a fabulous show played to a full house. She manifested her vision.

The only thing that stops you manifesting your dreams is your doubt and your fear. If you give twenty percent focus to what you want, you will achieve twenty percent of your dream. If you give one hundred percent quality focus to the outcome that you want you will have a one hundred percent outcome. The Law of Attention is exact.

Watch where you put your thoughts.

If you are driving you pay attention to the road ahead or you might crash. You watch the signposts so that you do not go in the wrong direction. When you focus on your driving you get safely to your destination or, in life, to your destiny. As we travel the road of life we are asked to pay attention to the whispers and hints with which the Universe signs our way.

If you give attention to a worry or fear you energise it and bring it into creation. Churning worst case scenarios in your mind or continually talking about your fears are powerful ways of drawing them into your life.

A client of mine lived in great anxiety because she constantly pictured her marriage breaking up. The attention she paid to the failure of her relationship programmed her unconscious mind to act in such a way as to break up the partnership. The Universe, of course, supported this by throwing challenging situations into her way. Her partner too was constantly picking up her psychic messages of fear and separation, which caused him to withdraw.

THE LAW
. . . . OF . . . .
ATTENTION

Inevitably the relationship ended. She fulfilled her own prophecies.

If you have a pain in your big toe and you focus on it, worry about it and churn over horrible possibilities, it assumes huge proportions and gets worse. If you receive a phone call bringing exciting news it diverts your attention from your toe and the pain disappears.

The positive has a more powerful charge than the negative.

Focus on, think about and talk about positive situations. When you hold the positive in your attention, you make your dreams come true.

If you are writing a book, painting a picture, building a house or involved in any project, keep the perfect finished result in your mind. When you hold the vision and do the necessary work, success is assured. Decide on your vision, commit to it, do the necessary work, give it full attention and you will be amazed how your life blossoms.

Here is a little word of caution. When you plant a seed you have a picture of a beautiful plant appearing at the appropriate time. Then you water it and look after it. However, you do not dig it up constantly to check that it is OK.

So pay attention to your vision but do not analyse
it to death.

*Focus on what you want
and you will get it.*

CHAPTER TEN

THE LAW OF FLOW

We live in a Universe comprised of energy, which flows like a river. Nothing is static. Everything moves. Nothing and no one is separate or untouched by others. This is why a polar bear cannot sneeze in the Arctic without a grain of sand moving in the Sahara and why loving yourself a little more affects a total stranger at the other end of the world.

When a river flows there are no empty spaces. If the flow is blocked the river eventually overflows. Water represents emotions. If emotions are blocked they stagnate so that relationships become stuck and stilted. This is because the blocked flow has become a stagnant pool. It is exhilarating to walk by a torrent but it may be dangerous to swim in it in case you are swept away. If your emotions are a torrent then people may be frightened to come too close to you in case they drown.

However, if a river is peaceful and serene then people want to sit by it. They want to enjoy the peace, serenity and tranquillity. It is safe to bathe here. If your emotions are peaceful, tranquil and serene many will want to come very close to you. Because they will want to bathe in your aura your personal relationships will be good.

So watch the flow of your emotions and notice the effect it has on your relationships.

The Law of Flow governs every area of life.

A torrent of sexuality may be exciting but it is threatening and dangerous to get sucked into.

Where sexuality is blocked by childhood prohibitions or past life experiences, a sexual relationship is uncomfortable. If your sexuality is flowing beautifully your sex life will be good.

Does your creativity flow or is it blocked? Is your creativity a torrent of fast-flowing ideas that get jumbled up and end up crashing on the rocks? Or does your creativity flow at a pace that you and those around you can handle, keeping you full of ideas and happily productive?

If a cupboard is crammed full, nothing new can be put into it. If you hoard, whether it is money, clothes, ideas or old resentments, there is no space for new to come in. To allow new into your life you must let go of the old.

If you hold on to old emotions you are full of those old memories which prevent fresh and happier things from coming in. As soon as you throw away rubbish from your home the Law of Flow will ensure that something else takes its place. It is your choice whether you replace rubbish with more rubbish or shift your consciousness to attract something better. If you have the same thoughts then the same conditions will return. If you start making changes, however small, then automatically something different has to come in.

Nature does not allow a vacuum, so something always moves into an empty space. Your task is to ensure it is something better.

As soon as you release beliefs and memories that are no longer needed in your life you open the gates for new to flood in. Change habits in order to bring something different into your life. It may be as simple as walking another way to work.

I was talking to a friend who decided that she was ready for a relationship. She hadn't had a relationship for a long time. I looked at her bedroom and it was absolutely full of clutter. I just raised my eyebrows and she said, 'You are right.' She cleared out all the clutter from her bedroom with the result that a relationship galloped into her life.

According to Feng Shui every part of your house relates to a different aspect of your life. If you have clutter or rubbish in the part of your house that relates to fame, then you prevent that aspect of your life from flowing. Different places relate to work, success, relationships, money and so on. In the same way, if there is an old belief cluttering up your life, clear it out. If there is an old memory sitting within you like a boulder, write it down and burn the paper to clear it away.

When you are physically clearing rubbish out of your house start affirming for what you wish to replace it. Start visualising a higher energy coming into your life so that something new and more joyous flows towards you.

Never clear out as a passive act. Do it with the energy that says, 'I am ready now for new in my life. This is what I want.'

Be masterful and use the Law of Flow to make your life what you want it to be.

Relationships prosper when there is a flow of open communication.

Prosperity results when we balance the outflow with the inflow.

*Go with the flow and you
will reach the source.*

CHAPTER ELEVEN

THE LAW OF ABUNDANCE

Abundance means flowing with love, joy, happiness, prosperity, success, vitality, laughter, generosity and all the good of life.

Our life becomes abundant when we flow with the higher qualities of life.

Your natural birthright is to flow with abundance for that is the divine wish for us all. Only one thing can stop you from receiving open-hearted generosity from Source – your consciousness. The flow of abundance is directed towards you but your thoughts, beliefs, memories and levels of deservingness create barriers to receiving it.

If you have a beautiful rose bush in your garden with a creeper sucking out its life force, it is not abundant. It may glow with glorious flowers for the moment but they will not be replaced unless you remove the creeper that is stopping the flow of vitality. A good gardener will remove the plant which is strangling the rose bush so that it can continue to flower gloriously. It is up to you to remove the beliefs which strangle your abundance.

Love is about enjoying all your relationships. We block our due abundance of love when we close our hearts. The creeper of our beliefs and fears about rejection and hurt gets a stranglehold on our heart. It causes us to cling on to relationships or to withdraw. We stop loving when our mind takes over and we see the imperfection of the other. Then we connect ego to ego. Your ego is the fear of your lower personality, and this forms boulders which block the flow of love.

Being in love is seeing the Divine in another and connecting soul to soul. This allows our passion to flow. A couple in love, a mother loving her new baby, colleagues sparking each other with ideas, friends immersed in the same interests, all glow with love. Everyone around them smiles for there is no more magnetic energy than being in love. Source *is* love so there is no shortage. Love flows from the heart of God to all of us, so open your heart for an abundance of love.

Success is a state of mind, not a particular achievement. When your all is focused on reaching a specific goal, nominated as success, there is a moment of elation at the moment of achievement. Then you have to set another one and strive again.

So success is not about trying to push a river, which just leads to stress, frustration and lack of self worth. Abundant success is about flowing with life, taking advantage of the currents and enjoying your journey.

True success is a sense of satisfaction and fulfilment.

I remember visiting a friend who refused to allow anyone to look after her even though she was ill. When she recovered her friends told her how frustrating they found this. She shared how much she had wanted to be nurtured and cared for but somehow could not bring herself to let it happen. Independence is a wonderful quality. However it is also appropriate to let people in to nurture us. It is part

of the give and take of flowing. The more we allow ourselves
to receive, the better we feel inside. Then, feeling full and
content within, we are genuinely able to nurture others.

When you consistently eat nourishing meals which keep
your blood-sugar level balanced, you don't crave sweets. When
you allow yourself to be nurtured regularly, you don't yearn
with neediness. When there is a natural in- and out-flow
of caring and nurturing in our lives we feel balanced and
abundant in love.

As above so below. Wise Earthly parents will give you
what you want when they think you are ready for it. No wise
parent gives a beautiful and delicate china doll to a toddler
because the child is quite likely to smash it or pull out its
hair. This will not be malicious but simply because the child is
not mature enough to care for such a gift. However much the
toddler clamours for a china doll like her sister's, the parents
will wait until they judge her to be ready to care for the doll
appropriately. It is the same in the heavens. However much
you clamour for the abundance you seek, the Universe will
not bring it to you until you prove that you are ready to
accept it.

The Law of Abundance is very simple. If you want more
friendships in your life, be friendly to others. Pull out the
boulders of suspicion, boredom or hurt that have blocked
your flow of friendliness.

If you want more happiness in your life, remember
that the thoughts, beliefs or memories that make you feel
sad are past. They have no reality at this moment. Prac-
tise smiling.

If you want more caring and nurturing in your life remove
the barriers that stop you from receiving it. When you are

open to receiving, people around you will automatically nurture you.

Material things flow to you when you have abundance consciousness.

Abundance is your birthright. Open up to receive it.

CHAPTER TWELVE

THE LAW OF CLARITY

When you are totally clear about what you want everyone picks up your message accurately and responds accordingly.

A young man I know called John managed to string out a relationship with his girlfriend for a long painful time by giving her mixed messages. He would turn up to see her saying he just wanted to be friends and then he would stay the night. If she needed him to help with her children or round the house, he simply could not say 'no'. He would say to all his friends, 'But I've made it perfectly clear that I'm not interested.' They all told him he was sending mixed messages. It certainly was not clear to Anita. She absolutely adored him and was ready to read that he loved her into everything he did or said.

It took over a year for her to realise that he did not want a committed relationship with her. She suffered a year of anxiety in a pull-push, on-off situation which really knocked her confidence. And then she still had to go through the grief of the separation. During that time her psychic energy was tied up in worry, false expectations and anger. His energy was tied up in anxiety and guilt.

Lack of clarity ties up psychic energy and keeps you in confusion. Clarity frees you to move forward and opens new doors.

Paul had lived with Jeanne for years. At first they had been very close but for the past two years he had felt quite alienated from her. He was seeing someone else with whom he was very much in love. Jeanne suspected this and raged at him constantly. He wanted to leave her but he simply could not tell her the truth. He told me that he could not bring himself to tell Jeanne that he did not love her anymore. The result was that Paul, Jeanne and his new lady were metaphorically living in a muddy pond and no one could see a way out. The future was full of confusion.

It was only when Paul took a decision to move out no matter what the consequences that clarity became possible. Jeanne at last knew where she stood. She changed her job and met a new man. Paul felt free at last and able to breathe for himself. He decided to live alone and give himself space to find out who he was again. His lover gave him the space he needed with the result that it freed her energy to focus on her studies.

Clear decisions move you from stuckness to freedom.

When we are worrying and our thoughts are going round and round in circles imagining every possible outcome, we are in the dark. Imagine there is a light which switches on over your head when you are ready to do something. If you are considering starting a business, while you are still examining the possibilities, the light is off. As soon as you are clear that you will do it, you say, 'This is the business I intend to start.' The light over your head switches on.

The moment you make a clear decision a light goes on over your head. The Powers That Be in the Universe see this light and align behind you to manifest your vision.

THE LAW
OF
CLARITY

If you are out walking in a thick fog you can very soon move off your path and can quickly get extremely lost. You may go round in circles regarding people, situations or your own personal anxieties and have no idea which direction to go in.

There are two ways to activate the Law of Clarity. If you have wandered off your path, are lost, frustrated and cannot see which way to go because of the thick fog, wait patiently until the sun clears the fog and you can see where you are. Then the direction becomes very clear to you.

If, on the other hand you are in a basin where there is permanent fog, with the result that you have been walking round and round in circles for a long time, take a decision to move in any direction.

It is imperative that you take a decision, however fearful or difficult, *but feel your way carefully* until you are in the clear.

The word 'decision' comes from the Latin *decedere*, meaning to cut off. A decision cuts you off from other possibilities. You must then focus on the route you have chosen. The quickest way to move along your spiritual path is to take clear decisions and implement them. Clarity opens doors to your future.

Truthfulness, honesty, genuineness, integrity are qualities of clarity. Other people pick this up and respond to you because they trust you.

Speak clearly to the Universe about your wants and needs. If you mumble or do not know what you want, you send a jumbled message to the great warehouse in the sky and may receive some surprising things you did not think you had ordered. Clear thoughts and intentions draw from the Universe that which you require in your life. Never forget.

You are a master. It is your right to order what you need and to expect your order to be fufilled.

Clarity is the first step to freedom and the achievement of your heart's desire.

CHAPTER THIRTEEN

THE LAW OF INTENTION

If you want to go swimming, you can be deflected. If you intend to swim, you will overcome all obstacles in order to fulfil your intention. Similarly, the person who intends to write a book is much more likely to succeed than the person who hopes to write one. Intentions are more powerful than wants, wishes or hopes. Intention releases a force that makes things happen.

Imagine an archer. He pulls his bow back and holds it 'in tension' as he aims at his target before unleashing the arrow. Whatever your aim in life, if you gather the energy and sight your target, the might of the Universe is unleashed behind your vision. Even if you do not actually accomplish your intention you have set a powerful force in motion.

A man told me that he had been owed a sum of money for some considerable time. Week after week he procrastinated about taking action. Because he was a compassionate person he could see the other person's difficulty. However, one day he decided he was going to pursue the money. He intended to go for it. That afternoon he wrote a clear letter to the lady with the outstanding debt. Half an hour later, before he had posted it, she phoned him and said the cheque would be in the post that day. He received it the following morning.

If you intend to send someone healing at a certain time, the force goes out at that time whether or not you do the absent healing at that moment.

The power of intention was clearly demonstrated to me

recently. I held an Angel Day in London. Our intention was to create a great column of light so that angels could access London through this high vibration, then spread love and light through England into the world. Because angels are high-frequency spiritual beings they find it difficult to lower their vibrations sufficiently to enter dark places. They can access such places more easily when we build bridges of light for them to move along. Before the event people called me from all over the world to say that individually and in groups they would be tuning into Angel Day to add their energy.

This was during the height of the war in the Balkans. Elizabeth, a mutual friend, told me that Tom Spencer, the Euro MP, would be in Macedonia on Angel Day itself. He is Chairman of the Foreign Affairs Committee of the European Parliament and intensely involved in the affairs of the Balkans. She contacted him.

These are his words:

'I and my Committee had watched the tragedy unfold and were determined to do what we could to help. I therefore arranged a conference of all the Chairmen of all the Foreign Affairs Committees and for two days parliamentarians from twelve countries, including the Albanians, wrestled with the fear which grips the region. At lunchtime on Sunday we piled into a coach to return across the mountains to Skopje, the capital of Macedonia. I had forgotten, in the pressure of events, my undertaking to Elizabeth, and thus to Diana, to concentrate during Sunday afternoon on the Angel Day meeting taking place so many miles away in London.

'The coach dropped some of the participants in Skopje but many of us drove north-west towards the Stankovic Camp. The afternoon was grey and cold. The coach edged its way across fields to the barbed-wire perimeter. Desperate groups of Albanians already living in Macedonia were shouting through the wire to try and establish contact with relatives and friends inside the camp.

'The camp had been built at immense speed by British soldiers. 50,000 people existing in immaculately erected lines of white tents. The Macedonian government, fearful of the destabilisation of its own fragile unity, was insisting that the new waves of Kosovar Albanians should not merge with their own Albanian population and were guarding the perimeter.

'The atmosphere was both physically and emotionally dark. The smell of 50,000 people with few washing facilities was overpowering. The anxious faces on both sides of the gate told the story of the terror of the previous three weeks. Attached to the wall of a hut, that had once been intended as the site of a new airport for Skopje, scraps of paper and lists of names told the story of a whole people desperately trying to find each other after the holocaust of expulsion.

'As the bus nudged its way through the crowded gate, a real sense of dread enveloped us. What should a suited politician say in the face of such suffering? Silently we clambered out and walked into the crowds. We were swamped by a sea of anxious faces asking for news, for advice and for hope. For half an hour the litany of ghastly stories poured forth. Each story told with immense dignity and an extraordinary lack of anger. Relatives murdered, families broken, lives up-turned. In small groups we wandered down the immense aisles between the tents.

'Then something wonderful happened. The clouds cleared, an extraordinary light suffused the camp. Suddenly it was a warm and pleasant evening. The atmosphere came to resemble a cross between an agricultural show and a promenade, so typical of the Mediterranean. In the corners of the camp, flags flew over the military hospitals established by the Germans, the Taiwanese and the Israelis. The four-wheel-drive vehicles of a dozen charities crawled through the drying mud.

'By now the camp was alive with people walking arm in arm, talking as if their lives had merely been disturbed for a brief moment. There was laughter, there was warmth, there was dignity. A NATO helicopter flew over. A Kosovar journalist spoke to me of the extraordinary kindness of the British soldiers who had built the camp. "They worked twenty-four hours a day and yet still had time to smile and play with the children."

'The mood of the camp was now almost exultant. Young men were playing basketball, women sat in corners talking of the future. The great camp with no central organisation moved and heaved like a great single entity. The stark beauty of the mountains, which before had seemed so threatening, were now bathed in the light of the setting sun. We climbed back into our coach and left the camp, full of determination and hope. I and half a dozen colleagues were put into a mountain-top hotel, looking down on Skopje. In the distance you could see a few lights picking out the perimeter of the camp. Only then did I remember my commitment to Angel Day. I checked the timing and it was absolutely precise. I had done nothing other than be there, but I have no doubt that the Light knew what it was doing.'

I believe that Tom Spencer's intention to anchor the light created an entry point for the bridge of light we were sending out from London. Many angels took the opportunity to use it.

Never underestimate the power of intention. A lady told me that she had lost touch with her brother. They had quarrelled some time ago because she did not like the fact that he was to marry again. She never met the new wife but prejudged her. Several years passed and she began to regret the things that she had said. She did some personal development work and realised that her bitterness about her brother was eating away at her and making her ill. At last she made the firm intention of letting it all go. One evening she sat quietly and talked to her brother as if he was in front of her. She told him how sorry she was for all that she had said and wished him much happiness. That night she had a very vivid dream in which her brother came to introduce his wife to her. They smiled and told her they were happy. She woke feeling happier than she had done in years, knowing that even if they never met again physically, all was well between them.

Intention is taken into consideration when assessing karma,

the balance sheet of our thoughts and deeds, with its inevitable consequences. A child runs out into the road in the path of a car and is injured. Does the driver bear karmic responsibility? It depends on his intention. If he was driving sensibly he does not. He has attracted lessons and possibly an initiatory incident to test himself. On the other hand, if he was drunk or angry or driving carelessly, he does bear responsibility at a spiritual level and will have to repay in some form.

If someone has evil intent, for example if they are focused on hurting, harming or creating havoc, a black mark is earned in their soul records. They are unleashing poisoned arrows. It does not matter whether they actually perpetrate the damage or not. The intention has gone out into the Universe and been noted.

When your intentions are noble and honourable, even if your plan does not come to fruition you will be rewarded for the purity of your ideals.

There is an expression, 'The road to hell is paved with good intentions'. This means that the arrow has been aimed but the string has not been pulled back and held in tension. There is no energy. Therefore nothing happens. The arrow does not fly. Sometimes the aim is wrong and the arrow misses the target. The Sanskrit root of the verb *sinnen* means to aim at a target and miss.

If your intention is clear but nothing seems to be happening, you may be held up for a reason. Imagine this. You are looking at your target. You have held the bow up and aimed but an animal runs between you and the target. The watchers are shouting 'Wait'. You drop your bow, wait and start again. There is always a higher reason for holding back.

If I ask for guidance, my angels and guides often say, 'What is your intention?' It is the intention that signals the rightness or otherwise of a project or an idea. Make sure that your intentions do not come from the ego but are for the highest good. Universal energy supports intention. It is the basis of manifestation.

A mission statement is the intention of the organisation clearly set out. Reading the mission statement aloud at the start of meetings keeps the target in the sights. Research indicates that companies who do this before business meetings achieve their objectives more quickly and completely than those who do not.

 An intention is like an arrow in flight. Nothing can deflect it. So aim carefully.

CHAPTER FOURTEEN

THE LAW OF PROSPERITY

Every parent wants their beloved child to have plenty. The divine Source, father/mother God, is no different. You are a beloved child of the Universe. It is time now for you to claim your divine heritage and be prosperous.

Some things hold you in lack and others allow you to prosper.

Take a plant. If you put it into inappropriate soil in a place which is full of slugs, with too much or too little water and sun, would you expect it to flourish? If you constrict its roots and space for growth, never feed it or constantly replant it, you will expect it to perish. So you plant it in good soil with enough water and sun. You give it freedom to grow and the safety to establish itself. You also protect and take care of it. You encourage it to flourish.

The spiritual laws which cause you to wither or flourish are the same. An unhelpful mindset is like poor soil. If you believe you do not deserve prosperity, that is stony ground. A belief in yourself is rich, fertile soil. Fear and apathy dry you up while enthusiasm, joy and expectation enable you to expand.

Express yourself creatively. Give yourself freedom to develop. Cultivate your gifts and talents. Your prosperity will flourish.

We draw from the universal pool according to our consciousness. You either have poverty consciousness or abundance consciousness. Many aspirants have in previous

lives been in religious orders where they have taken vows of
poverty. This was appropriate then, but if it is still active now
it is not serving them for they will feel guilty about having
money. If you suspect this applies to you, pray for the release
of the vow or vows or make an appointment with a spiritual
therapist who can help you release them.

Most old souls do not value material things to the same
extent as younger souls. This is understandable because they
have chased after the material in past lives and know it to be
illusory. Sometimes they lose the plot and feel that material
things are unspiritual. Far too many nice people think it is
ungodly to have money. Quite the reverse is true.

*The most spiritual thing is to have money and use it wisely
with love.*

Huge fear underlies poverty consciousness. I receive frantic, terrified letters from people who are at their wits' end
about their financial situation. All their available energy is
tied up in their focus on lack.

It is not spiritual to keep worrying about money.

Greed is financial indigestion. It is the equivalent of being
invited to a buffet and piling your plate up high with more
than you could possibly want to satisfy your hunger. It makes
you ill or somehow blocks your energy.

If you hoard money in the bank without letting it flow,
you eventually tell the Universe that you don't want more
and eventually it stops sending.

'He who knows he has enough is rich,' says Lao Tzu (Taoism). *The spiritual ideal is to have enough and know that is plenty.*

There was a man with a chip on his shoulder who was always complaining. He was lazy and he felt unworthy. He missed opportunities because he did not believe in himself. He was unhappy and poor. If you are mean-spirited, rigid-minded and tight-fisted you will never feel contented or happy for poverty consciousness is an attitude.

Those who are generous-hearted, open-minded and giving will always be contented and happy. Their attitude of prosperity consciousness will ensure this.

The legendary Paul Getty was rich beyond most people's imagination. He was worth billions and was surrounded by material riches, but he lived alone and in constant fear of loss. He was a rich man with poverty consciousness.

Prosperity means having a sense of financial wellbeing.

Many of the pharoahs, Joseph of Egypt, countless great and wealthy rulers have been highly evolved Masters who have undertaken the responsibility of riches. The lesson of prosperity is to use riches with wisdom.

Wealth bestows responsibility and power.

There is a well-known story about a wise and bountiful ruler. The King had four children, who he adored. Eventually they grew up and each went out into the world to explore and seek their fortunes. Their father hoped they would all return one day with experiences to share and new knowledge and wisdom.

Years passed and the King began to think they would never return. Then one day a ragged beggar appeared at the gates and announced she was his daughter. On being told of this the horrified King rushed to the gates, to discover it really was his child.

'How have you sunk to this?' he cried in distress. 'Come in, my beloved daughter.'

He brought her into the palace and ordered new clothes and a banquet in her honour. But she would have none of it. She did not think she was worthy of his kingdom and preferred to spend her days begging, whining and complaining outside the palace gates. Her father was devastated.

Some time passed before a young man appeared at the palace gates stating he was the King's son. Overjoyed, the father hurried to greet him and again ordered a banquet and fine clothes. To his consternation his son appeared to have forgotten his birthright. The King found him scrubbing steps like a servant. His son said he was unworthy to receive the bounty of the kingdom. His attitude was totally servile. He had to do things all the time to justify his keep. His father was distressed.

Months went by until one day a beautiful lady in a carriage drawn by six white horses entered the gates, announcing she was the King's daughter. She was taken to the King, who was overjoyed that his beloved daughter had returned at last. She enjoyed the banquet and all the finery of being a princess but when he asked her to help him with his work of ruling the kingdom, she said, 'No. It is your kingdom, Father. You run it.' She wanted bounty without responsibility. The father was deeply concerned.

Finally the fourth child returned. He was a fine young man with clear eyes and a strong face. The old King rejoiced to see him. The young man enjoyed the banquet and the abundance of his position as his father's son. He toured the kingdom. Then he said to his father, 'I have returned with new ideas and suggestions. How can I help?'

'My son,' replied the King. 'I wish you to rule by my side and take responsibility with me for the kingdom.'

'Gladly,' responded his son.

His father smiled and relaxed. He was delighted.

True prosperity comes when we accept our bountiful birthright and the responsibility and power that this entails.

Think, speak and act as if you are prosperous and you will impress the Universe to send you plenty.

CHAPTER FIFTEEN

THE LAW OF
MANIFESTATION

You have manifested every single thing that is in your life. You may have used the Laws of Attention, Attraction, Prayer or any one of the spiritual laws I have already described to bring these things to you. Most of this is done unconsciously.

Spiritual aspirants who tune into information and guidance from angels and higher Beings of Light and who master their minds and emotions, can manifest intentionally.

We live in an ocean of divine consciousness flowing with the symbols of our heart's desire. That which you wish to draw into your life is already swimming in the ether of the unmanifest world like a beautiful fish waiting for you to reel it in. Each fish has a frequency of its own and is broadcasting on the celestial waveband. Your first task is to tune into the vibrational frequency of the vision you seek. This is to access the information you need to draw it into your life.

Fish swimming in the celestial seas emit sounds of a high frequency. You must send out a matching note in order for them to come to you.

Your constant thoughts send out interference which stop you fine-tuning to the frequency you need to be able to hear. It is like trying to catch that fish while splashing about in the water. Sounds of talking, boat engines, hooters, the noise of the world interfere with your ability to tune into the message of the fish.

If you are swimming in murky water the fish is unlikely to approach you or you may not see it if it does. Get into pure water by stilling your mind.

Be certain you know which sort of fish you really want. Otherwise you may find yourself catching a shark. Clarity is a key to manifestation.

Be still and clear, raise your frequency to that of whatever you want, then it will approach you. If you wish to have a friend who is open hearted, fun loving and light, you must develop those qualities in yourself.

The ability to manifest is a mighty power, so it is imperative that you manifest only for the highest good. Therefore the first step is to meditate and listen to your inner guidance, so that you are totally clear what you intend to manifest.

As soon as you have clarity, picture what you want. Visualisation is an important key, for pictures enter the right brain, which is the mighty creative computer.

You must have absolute total faith that it is on its way. Do not doubt. Do not deviate. Hold the vision.

When you are a high-dimension being like Jesus Christ you can bring loaves and fishes from the unmanifest dimension to the material by the power of your clear vision and faith. Sai Baba, the avatar who lives in India, does the same. He manifests beautiful jewellery and also *vibhutti* healing ash for his devotees. I understand that there are many gurus and also magicians who have this power. They tune into the fish they want which then swims into their hands.

While some fifth-dimensional people can manifest with

the power of thought alone, third or fourth-dimensional people have to take action in order to manifest.

I was talking about manifestation to my daughter and she said, 'Remind people to start small.' She told me how she had manifested a tissue for herself that morning.

She was walking into town to go to the library when her nose started to run. She did not have a handkerchief or a tissue on her and she certainly did not want to buy a box of tissues and carry it round town. So she decided to manifest a tissue. Now she was totally clear that she wanted one! She knew that God wanted her to have one too. So somewhere there was a tissue for her. She absolutely knew without doubt that a tissue was going to be provided for her in a perfect way, so she kept an eye open for it. When she walked into the library there was a box of tissues just under the counter, so she took action and asked for one. The librarian said, 'Have as many as you like, love.'

There is no difference between manifesting a tissue and manifesting something bigger. The key is our faith in our ability to do it.

If clarity is your difficulty, write down exactly what you want. If you want a partner, write in detail the qualities you wish him or her to have. This gives information to your left brain computer, your logical mind. Relax and visualise this person, so that your right-brain computer, your creative mind, is working in synchronicity with your left.

Then make sure you have matching qualities within you. If you want an open, warm-hearted person, check that you are open and warm-hearted.

If you wish to manifest a car, write down exactly what you need. Picture it. Then make sure you are sending out the vibrations which match the vibration of that car. If you have small-car consciousness, it is no use trying to manifest a Rolls-Royce.

You must be able to feel the good feeling of having what you are manifesting. Focus on the higher qualities of that which you wish to manifest and then align with them. If having a particular job would give you a sense of satisfaction, focus on that feeling of satisfaction. Do things that bring you satisfaction until your inner feeling aligns with that of the job on offer. Then it manifests for you.

One way to cast the line for your fish is to draw on a piece of paper exactly what you want. Make sure the energy is right, so be careful of the colours you use, for each colour has a vibration. Write on your picture, 'This or something better now manifests for the highest good of all.' You may have asked for a sprat while the Universe is ready to offer you a mackerel.

Now that you have baited your line with the bait attractive to your fish, go for a walk and wait for the fish to approach. In other words, detach from your desire. Then come back and take whatever action is necessary to bring it in.

Om is the sound of creation. Sound has a vibration. Some sounds shatter. Others heal. *Om* purifies, stills and manifests. When you have taken the above steps picture your vision while you *om*. This accelerates its manifestation. Different traditions spell this om, ohm or aum.

Here is a resumé of the steps needed to activate the Law of Manifestation.

1. Be still and listen.
2. Be very clear about what you want.
3. Relax and visualise yourself receiving it.

4. Align your vibration to what you wish to manifest.
5. Have total faith it is on its way.
6. Hold your vision and *om* for its manifestation.
7. Take any necessary action.

 Cast your line into the celestial oceans.
Align your frequency
to that of your vision
and it will manifest into
your reality.

CHAPTER SIXTEEN

THE LAW OF SUCCESS

In material terms success simply means achieving your desired outcome. Whether this is for bad or good the same laws apply for the universal energy will support your free will.

The easiest way to achieve material success is to use the Law of Attention. Be clear about what you want, have the necessary confidence and determination, then work steadfastly towards that vision. Focus on it ceaselessly. If you are using this law in order to achieve your aim you cannot afford a single negative thought. More importantly you cannot afford a single negative picture.

Your beliefs create an energy which vibrates around you. Success follows when you believe in yourself. Watch your beliefs and carefully prune out those that do not help you towards your goals.

For success in love watch your beliefs about love. Those that create success are: 'I am lovable, I trust people, I respond lovingly to other people's overtures, I open my heart and give generously of myself, I relax and believe I am lovable.'

Beliefs that result in business success are: 'I can trust people, I deserve to succeed, I deserve to have good things, I can handle anything.'

In spiritual terms success means believing in yourself, doing the best you can and achieving the highest outcome for everyone.

Success comes when we get the energy right. My understanding is that Sai Baba is the highest-vibration being on the planet at this time. Thousands of people flock to his ashram every day for the *dharshan* or blessing that his presence confers. On most days he walks through the crowds who are sitting cross-legged in silence on the floor of the temple. He collects letters that devotees hand to him. Some he takes. Others he ignores. If he takes your letter, your request is blessed. Those who have their letter accepted are naturally delighted. It signals to them that they have got the energy of their request right.

Often those who fail to have their letters accepted are bitter and disillusioned. This comes from a misunderstanding of spiritual law. If their request is not spiritually right, how can they expect to have it blessed?

A friend of mine called Kevin stayed for a couple of weeks at Sai Baba's ashram in Puttaparthi. He wrote out his letter asking for a blessing on the next step of his life as he saw it. Although Sai Baba walked past him and took the letters of those on either side of him, Kevin's letter was ignored. He was surprised but did not despair. He knew that he must meditate quietly until he got it right. After meditation, he wrote another letter, slightly different from the first. This too was ignored. Once more he prayed and meditated before a flash of illumination came to him and he was able to see many things from a different perspective. With this in mind he wrote a third letter coming from the heart (love) rather than the ego (desire). As Sai Baba graciously took this letter, he smiled at Kevin who knew that he could now move forward in life with divine blessing.

Success occurs when our personal or collective vibration resonates with the vibration of the wished-for outcome.

When you are congruent people trust your aura of integrity. So if you speak what you believe and 'walk your talk' you will create success as long as it is positive.

You hold your thoughts in your left brain and pictures in your right brain. Pictures are more powerful than thoughts. If you think success but picture failure, you will fail. Furthermore, when your thoughts and pictures are in opposition, two powerful aspects of you are fighting. This leads to depression, exhaustion and confusion.

> *When your left and right brain are congruent so that you think successful thoughts and picture success, success with harmony is inevitable.*

If success arrives on your lap from nowhere then it is karma, the reward for work done in a past life being reaped in this one. Karma has placed you in the right place, at the right time, with the appropriate mindset. It is the inevitable result of the energy you have invested during your soul's journey over lifetimes. It is the same whether you are working for evil and have a negative vision, such as robbing a bank, or working for the light by helping people for the highest good. The difference is this: success in bad things creates debts which will inevitably have to be repaid, some place, some life. Then you will feel you are being dogged by bad luck. Success in good things accelerates your soul's journey towards ascension. Your life is smiled on by fortune. Good luck and lucky breaks are the results of good karma.

In order to succeed you must also follow the Law of Flow. A wheel cannot turn if it is rusted up. The rust has to be cleaned out before the vehicle can move forward.

If you wish to activate the Law of Success and allow the wheel of fortune to turn for you, let go of the old and keep a positive focus on where you wish to be.

To succeed, clear out the physical, mental and emotional clutter.

You cannot succeed if you do not know where you are going. If you wish to cross the sea to the continent, you make certain preparations before you set off. You decide on your proposed destination, for example, whether you are heading for Marseilles or Calais. There is always flexibility to change direction later on. You examine and take account of the wind and currents. You load up the boat with necessary provisions. When you decide to get going you switch on the engine. Too many people do not succeed because they spend all their time planning their journey but never start. Finally you raise the anchor. This means that you make a break with the old and take the risk of moving into a different future.

In spiritual terms success is measured by the sense of satisfaction and fulfilment it gives you.

If you have earned millions and are stressed out, you are not deemed successful in the eyes of spirit. Nor are you if you have climbed to the top of the pyramid but have harmed people in the process. Nor if you are the winner but your integrity is compromised.

You are successful when you have achieved your aim through co-operation and by empowering others.

*Success occurs when your
vibration resonates with
the vibration of the outcome
you desire.*

THE
LAWS OF
HIGHER
AWARENESS

CHAPTER SEVENTEEN

THE LAW OF BALANCE
AND POLARITY

When a child sits on a swing he moves up and down in an
ever-increasing arc until he has swung as far forward and back
as is possible. After experiencing this for as long as he needs
to he slows down and comes back to a point of balance and
stillness.

Our lifetimes are similar. We experience one aspect of
life and then its opposite. The more we wish to explore one
extreme the further from the centre we swing. Then we must
swing the other way to understand its opposite.

If we have lifetimes of riches we will need to experience
the opposite which is poverty. If we become a tyrant our
soul will wish us to compensate by being a victim. We
all have unresolved aspects within us and our aim is to
integrate the polarities so that we can live in balance. Because
consciousness is now moving forward very rapidly, instead of
taking lifetimes to get into balance, we are bringing forward
the different aspects of our personality and aiming to balance
them during this life.

Someone who is a manic-depressive is swinging from one
pole to the other to such an extent that he is out of control.
I knew a man who was sometimes a powerful, bullying,
overbearing ogre. When he had pushed people away from
him too far with his attitude, he became a pathetic victim
to draw them in again. These are polar positions. When he

balances these personalities he will no longer try to control. Instead he will accept and love himself and let others be themselves.

The person who is sometimes very generous and gives everything away, then becomes mean and withholding, is swinging between polarities. Their task is to be centred about money.

Another common polarity-swing is to be very angry and controlling, then be detached and aloof. These are opposite forms of control. The balance is to be open-hearted and even-tempered.

Bingeing and starving are opposite poles. They are a manifestation of feeling out of control and therefore trying to control whatever is possible.

Masculine energy is doing, thinking, logical, aggressive, while the feminine counterpart is being, creating, intuitive, passive. Our aim is to balance these internally so that we can listen to our intuition *and* act on it; we can have creative ideas *and* think them through to fruition. We can rest *and* play. We can nurture *and* protect. If any of these qualities is out of balance we are called on to recentre ourselves and make new life choices.

I had an interesting experience which was no doubt drawn to me to show me reflections of opposite polarities within me. I spent a couple of days with an old friend who is a counsellor and healer. She embodies the feminine principle. We swapped sessions and of course talked a great deal. She is extremely gentle and non-invasive. I felt very open and ready to reveal myself to her and left her feeling respected, empowered, nourished, strengthened. I felt I made many awarenesses and released old patterns.

THE LAW
OF
BALANCE AND POLARITY

Later in the week I spent a couple of days with another friend. She is very powerful, incisive and on a crusade to pull everyone's stuff out. She embodies the masculine principle of tough determination. Her insights are extraordinary and most helpful, yet I felt violated, disempowered, resistant and ungrateful. Even though I told her exactly how I felt, she disregarded this because her personal goal was more important than my feelings. Her personal goal was to pull out my negative patterns whether I gave her permission or not.

My task is to balance the part of me that is ruthlessly incisive with that which is nurturing and empowering.

If you do not like the way you were treated as a child very likely you will overcompensate with your own children. For example, if your parents were witholding and mean you may give your children more than you can afford. If they were overprotective you may let your children have too much freedom.

We are always seeking balance. When we find it the lesson is learnt. It is done for all time. Balancing aspects of our personality is rather like riding a bicycle. You fall off to one side and the other. Then you wobble. Eventually you balance and ride smoothly. Even if you do not ride a bike for years, you will be able to do so easily when you next try. A wobble or two, perhaps, but not the lurches you experienced when you first learnt.

This point of equilibrium is the balance which we seek in all things.

Our aim is to balance all
aspects of our lives.

CHAPTER EIGHTEEN

THE LAW OF KARMA

I first met Tom ten years ago and liked him immediately. He was always warm and friendly. He was really interested in people and loved to listen to them. Someone told me that even as a child he was kind and thoughtful. His life had certainly not been easy, but however bad things were for him he always found time for others.

When he was in his forties an opportunity arose for him to realise a lifelong dream to start a business. It meant that he and his wife would have to move to a new area and put up some capital. However, he did not have enough money to do it. Unexpectedly, at the eleventh hour, a neighbour who had looked after him sometimes when he was a child and who he had not seen for twenty years, died and left him a considerable sum of money. It was the exact amount he needed comfortably to start the new venture. The energy of thoughtfulness, kindness and goodness that he had always given out was converted by the Universe to the energy of money and returned to him at the right time. Tom received his just reward of good karma.

Hate and anger are damaging energies. When you send them out they too will return to you in some form. It may be as a dog bite, ill health, an accident or as someone hating you.

The law of karma is 'as you give so you receive'. Bad thoughts and deeds return to you. So does kindness, thoughtfulness, love, joy and generosity. To the exact extent that you live these qualities, you will *at some time* receive an equivalent back into your life. It may not be from the direction you sent it to.

Karma is recorded and balanced. Loving thoughts, emotions, words and deeds are credits. Negative ones are debits. The Universe calls these up when we least expect it. People unaware of karma call it fate or luck, good or bad.

It is always sensible to have a credit in the karmic bank to draw on in time of need. Think, speak and act for the highest good and you will be a 'lucky' person.

Your family is your karma. Your soul chooses your family before you are born. Difficult family ties may be a consequence of unresolved feelings or situations in a past life. You chose that family this time because you wanted another chance to resolve the problems. They offer you the lessons your soul needs to learn. Close, warm, loving feelings towards members of your family almost certainly mean that you had a loving bond with them in another life. You chose them to support you and give you a solid loving foundation for this one.

We call family members relations because our souls in consultation have decided we need to learn to relate to each other in this life. As humans we often refuse to accept the opportunities which our relatives offer us for growth and transmutation of karma. Instead we prefer to carry on the old vendettas or feelings of separation and irritation. I have often heard people say, 'We can choose our friends but not our families.' In fact our Higher Self chooses our families, while we choose our friends according to our personality.

I knew an old man who was extremely authoritarian. Throughout their long marriage he had kept his wife firmly under his thumb. Although there was a lot of love between them, he had always put her down and told her that she was not capable of doing things. Eventually she lost her confidence.

As she grew older she became somewhat senile, which gave her the excuse to do and say most outrageous things. She giggled as she did this, taking absolutely no responsibility for her words or actions. Sometimes she even physically attacked him. He was devastated. He no longer had any control over her.

When I was visiting them one day the old man's son said to me with a shrug, 'She's just getting her own back on him for all the years he was so awful to her.' A karmic situation was being played out.

Right at the end of their lives the husband became gentler and kinder to her. Despite her senile state she responded by being more responsible and loving. Love started to radiate from one to the other. It was beautiful to see. I hope that in those last weeks they healed the hurts and redressed the balance of karma so that if they incarnate together again they will be able to empower and love each other.

> *By loving and empowering others we heal karmic*
> *relationships.*

It is a pleasure to be with people who bring good karma into their marriages. An Indian lady who had an extremely happy arranged marriage told me that her husband was wonderful. She said they adored each other even after twenty-four years of marriage; that he was kind, generous, wise, supportive and hardworking, 'I know it was good karma

which brought him into my life,' she smiled radiantly. 'I
am blessed.'

*If you have a problem with someone, mentally wish them
well. This will start to heal the karma.*

Mindsets that you bring into this life with you are also
your karma. If you have a mindset that you are not good
enough, the belief will inevitably draw into your life things
and people that make you feel inferior.

Keith was the oldest child in the family and, like many
first children, he had a mindset that he was responsible for
everybody. He chose to incarnate as the oldest because it
enabled him to play out his karma. When he was quite
small his father said to him, 'You are to look after your
brothers and sisters.' Because this was in line with his belief,
he took this injunction very seriously. From that time on he
carried the burden for his brothers and sisters financially and
emotionally. As an adult he examined his belief and changed
his attitude. He realised that his mindset did not serve him
and it certainly did not serve his siblings. He set them free to
take responsibility for their own finances and emotions. This
freed him from the karmic burden he had been carrying and
released them to grow.

*You only carry karma until you have learnt the lesson.
Ignorance keeps you burdened. Free yourself now through
awareness and love.*

Positive beliefs create good karma. My friend Robin had

a belief that the Universe would always look after him. His relationship with his wife broke down and he had to move out of the family home. He had no money to pay rent but he met someone who invited him to share his home and they became great friends. Soon after this he went into hospital for an operation. A lady, who was almost a stranger, took him from the hospital into her beautiful home where she and her husband looked after him. He told me that when he looked back through his life, he had always been supported in unexpected ways. He said, 'I really trust that the Universe will look after me.' Positive beliefs create good karma in your life. Wonderful things then happen. You are responsible for your mindset so change your programmes if they do not serve you. You are the only person who can do it.

If your beliefs do not make you happy change them NOW.

Your health is your karma. Before you incarnated you chose your family, your life challenges and your mission. You also chose your body and your genetic predisposition. If for the growth of your soul you chose a family with a predisposition to an illness, the challenge that this provides becomes your karma. You may have chosen a family that has abundant health and a body that is strong and well. Then that is your karma. Your moment by moment choices of thoughts and emotions will affect your vitality and health. This is karma.

Jesus Christ described karma as 'you reap what you sow'. If you look after your seedlings carefully you get better plants. A healer told me that the children in her daughter's class at school planted beans on blotting paper. Her little girl held the bean in her hands and sent loving energy to it before she planted it. When the teacher asked her what she was doing, she replied, 'I'm giving my bean healing.' Apparently the results were quite astonishing. This bean grew more quickly and strongly than all the others.

There is an exact spiritual working-out for everything over our lifetimes. If somebody is accumulating large karmic debts for themselves by robbing houses, stealing cars or harming God's creation in any way, it is an act of compassion and common sense on the part of society to restrain that person. It means they can no longer build up debts which would make their subsequent lives more difficult.

The balance sheet of your karma is known as your akashic record. Your personal record is kept by your guardian angel, who is with you throughout all your lives and is also known as the recording angel. The Lords of Karma, who are incredibly evolved beings, are in charge of all akashic records, which are held in the great Universal computer. When you are offered an opportunity to incarnate, they help your soul to make important decisions, including your choice of parents and what you wish to learn and accomplish in your lifetime.

Karma is carried forward from lifetime to lifetime. We may not experience the consequences of our actions until a subsequent lifetime. Because of this there is often no obvious and visible correlation between an action and its consequence, with the result that many people have forgotten the Law of Cause and Effect. The higher our vibration the more quickly karma returns to us. If you feel that you never get away with anything you are subject to instant karma. This means that whatever you give out comes back to you instantly. It is a sign that you are becoming more evolved because your karmic balance sheet is being kept up to date. Your soul is no longer allowing you to accumulate debt.

It has now been decreed by God that it is time for karma to end on earth. You may access your akashic record, the balance sheet of your debts and credits over lifetimes, in meditation.

We are incredibly privileged to live now, for we can apply for a divine dispensation to free us from our karmic debt. This is the first time this has been available to souls on Earth. When you have done everything possible to heal a situation or relationship you may ask Source, in meditation, via the Lords of Karma, for divine dispensation to release the burden of your karma.

If you wish to enjoy a secure future pay back your spiritual debts and build up credit in the bank of the Universe.

 Remember that you reap what you sow.

CHAPTER NINETEEN

THE LAW OF
REINCARNATION

Carne means flesh. Incarnation is when our spirit enters a physical body. Reincarnation is the principle of returning into a physical body more than once. Under the Law of Reincarnation, if there is anything unresolved or incomplete at the end of a lifetime, your soul is allowed an opportunity to return in human form to resolve or complete it.

If you cheat your business partner your soul will wish to make amends by returning to help him or her in another life.

Where a husband has harmed his wife, they will wish to return together so that the soul of the husband can repay. They may reincarnate as husband and wife or parent and child, student and teacher or even as friends.

For example, a woman felt a compulsion to look after her chronically sick grandchild. She stayed with him all the time. During regression she realised that in a past life they had been husband and wife. In that life as a man he had abandoned the wife, who had suffered dire consequences. That wife was now the grandchild and this time she felt she had to stay with him.

If a parent dies leaving his children feeling angry, confused or misunderstood, under the Law of Reincarnation those spirits will choose to come back together to try to relate differently. Whole families often return at the same time in an effort to work things out. Communities who are in conflict or at war will come back to Earth together to see if their souls can find peace together instead of battle.

Often we reincarnate again and again into similar circumstances because of the soul's desire to put the past to rest. Once we are on Earth, in this material plane of free choice, it is all too easy to forget the ideals and perspective of the spiritual world. Once again we make the same mistakes and are trapped in the cycle of reincarnation.

As above so below. A child works its way through toddler group, kindergarten, infants', junior and senior school. As he grows up he goes to college, then university and finally may take a masters or Ph.D.

Earth is a learning establishment in which our lessons are presented to us in the form of experiences. The breaks, weekends, half-terms or holidays are known as death. We have a holiday in spirit before returning to school in the flesh. Just as a schoolchild and its parents scrutinise the report at the end of each term, we review each lifetime when we die. With the help of our guides, angels and spiritual mentors, known as the Lords of Karma, we decide which lessons we wish to brush up on and which classes we need to redo. Where we have done well, our soul learns new lessons in the following term.

Earthlings, those for whom Earth is a primary learning experience for their soul's journey, enter all the classes which Earth offers. They will experience lives in every religion, lives as soldiers, peasants, merchants, in the arts and every conceivable area they can learn from. These souls will incarnate again and again to perfect lessons and repay karma. They will experience all polarities, such as student and teacher, rich and poor, male and female, selfishness and service, the murderer and murdered, the betrayer and betrayed. The akashic records are the balance sheet of our lifetimes which are kept by the Lords of Karma. Good and bad are credits and debits. In future lifetimes we can call on our credit, but must also pay our debts.

There are many reasons for wishing to reincarnate.

To put right past wrongs, in other words to repay our debts.

To experience and strengthen ourselves.

To learn more about emotions, sexuality and other lessons only available on Earth.

To help, teach, be a light, or serve on this planet.

Because of its difficult conditions, Earth is a much prized teaching establishment in the Universe. Souls put their names down on a waiting list to get here because it offers opportunities for growth not available elsewhere. Every lesson here is to do with love.

This is the planet of free choice. Every thought, word or deed eventually manifests into your life. Your mindsets and emotions build your physical body and provide you with more experiences. Once you have mastered the lessons of the Earth plane your soul can serve in many of the higher light establishments of the universes.

Earth is the cosmic equivalent of a crocodile-infested swamp. Only intrepid souls sign on for this challenge. If you can get through it without getting muddy you are a hero. People often get stuck in the mud and then experienced souls offer to embody to help them. In so doing they too get contaminated and also have to return to repay Karma.

Now something new is happening. Earth is moving to a higher dimension. This means the mud in the swamp is drying up and all skeletons and rubbish are surfacing to be seen in the light of day. It is time now to look at our rubbish and clear it out.

Here is a simplistic overview.

Baby souls in their first incarnations will choose a very simple life. They may choose a simple society or a family where they are totally looked after. They often stay for only a few hours, days or weeks just to touch the atmosphere of Earth.

Toddler souls need clear instructions and boundaries. They cling to fundamentalist faiths and are anti-divorce or anything that breaks down a safe structure. They create much karma for themselves because of rigid control, dogmatism and missionary zeal.

Teenage souls go out into the world and sometimes create havoc. They also tend to get heavily into karmic debt because they often misuse their energy. However, they have the zest and life-force to get enterprises under way and start new things. They challenge the old ways.

Middle-aged souls are becoming wise and starting to repay debts they built up in early incarnations. They often have difficult lives because of this.

Old souls are wise and peaceful. However, they are often so distanced from the material that they do not tend to make a splash in the world.

There is ultimately a spiritual working-out of all things. If people only knew they must return to put right the wrongs of their life they might take heed of the spiritual laws. I feel that when the Roman Emperor Constantine the Great with his mother Helen had all reference to reincarnation deleted from the New Testament in AD 325 they did a disservice to Christianity. In AD 553 in Constantinople the Emperor Justinian confirmed this action and declared reincarnation a heresy, fearing that an understanding of the sacred Law of Reincarnation was weakening the growing power of the Church.

It is not up to us to judge what somebody else is doing or how they are handling the lessons of their incarnation. Just be aware that every single soul is on a journey over many lifetimes and they are learning on that journey.

Only a young soul will harm people, animals or the planet. Have compassion for young souls for they do not understand what they do. Ultimately they will have to repay what they have done to others. The task of an evolved soul is to help them without taking responsibility for them or patronising them. The greatest way of helping another is to demonstrate by example that there is another way of living.

Reincarnation strictly means 'coming back into the flesh'. However, many star people are incarnating now to help with the shift of consciousness taking place. Star people have come from different planets, sometimes different universes, where, of course, they do not have a physical body. There are many on Earth now who are from the Plaiedes, Saturn, Mars, Jupiter, Venus, Andromeda and other galaxies. Some are from more distant universes.

Star children are evolved souls who come to Earth to help. They have a different perspective on life. They are also here to experience and often they too become tarnished in the duality of Earth and earn karma. Then they wish to return to repay the debts. Generally they have less karma because they have had fewer incarnations and therefore less opportunity to accrue it.

Star people often have a sense of being different and feel

they do not belong here. If you find this Earth experience strange and difficult, if you cannot understand the folly and stupidity of humankind and know that life is a spiritual challenge not a material one, if you have a desire to serve, you are almost certainly a star child.

Star people and earthlings alike are deciding to take advantage of the windows of opportunity now opening for ascension. Ascension means raising your spiritual vibration to such a level that you do not need to reincarnate. For this you must have paid off your karmic debts, mastered the lessons of Earth and opened your heart and mind.

Once you have left the wheel of rebirth behind, you move into higher planes of the Universe, continuing to evolve in the light.

You return to Earth again *and again until you have mastered the spiritual laws.*

CHAPTER TWENTY

THE LAW OF RESPONSIBILITY

Responsibility is the ability to respond appropriately to a person or situation.

When the clarion call goes out for souls to undertake certain jobs, do you respond? Do you respond to your intuition and to visions you are sent? Challenges are sent by the Universe to check how you respond. Successive tests prepare you for spiritual promotion. It is up to you to prove that you can handle responsibility. Before promotion you must pass the tests, for many souls may be relying on you.

As above so below. As soon as you believe your child will drive your car safely you are happy to lend it to him. When a student is trusted to behave honourably and sensibly he is made a prefect. A business person is not promoted until he has demonstrated he can deal with likely problems.

When the Powers That Be believe that you can do a piece of work properly they will give you the responsibility for it.

There are certain times in life when we take on spiritual responsibilities. One is to bring a child into the world. Whether the baby is consciously planned or not, your Higher Self and the baby's Higher Self agreed to it. Your spiritual growth depends on how you respond to it. To bring a handicapped child into incarnation is an extra responsibility, providing you with more challenges and opportunities for growth if you choose to accept them.

When you head a great project or business, many souls will be affected by your decisions. For instance, if you are in charge of a school or a hospital, you are responsible for the welfare of many. If you rise with integrity to the challenge, your spiritual progress will be enhanced.

> *Challenges and responsibilities are an honour. They*
> *indicate that spiritually you are ready for greater*
> *things.*

Everything and everyone you are given to look after is a responsibility. If you do not respond to the challenge then it will be taken away from you and may be re-presented at another time.

Everything in your life is on loan to you. How do you look after your children, your home, garden, clothes and books? You have a responsibility to care for them.

You cannot take on great responsibility in life if you do not take care of your own needs. Your emotions and spirit need to be looked after. Your body is a temple which must be cared for. Take care of yourself first. Then you are in a fit state to help others.

However, with the exception of your small children, you are not responsible *for* anyone else. Every single individual is responsible for their own feelings and their own destiny and you do not have the right to carry someone else's burden for them for then you prevent their growth.

Your responsibility is to empower and strengthen others and encourage them to carry their own responsibilities.

A client of mine called Bernard was a charming if somewhat worried-looking young man. He had a mentally retarded sister. She was perfectly capable of looking after herself and could keep down a simple job. However, there were some things in our complex society that she clearly could not cope with. Her parents could not handle the responsibility of this young woman. They washed their hands of her and told their son that she was his responsibility. He accepted it. None of the other siblings wanted to know and he became overly protective of her. When he had to go away on an extended trip, he was extremely worried that she wouldn't be able to cope. He asked another sister to go down for the weekend and keep an eye on the girl. She declined, saying it was nothing to do with her. In the end he had to leave her to fend for herself. When he returned from his trip he discovered that she had done all the jobs around the house that he had been doing for years, thinking she was incapable. Furthermore she had called a plumber when her radiator leaked, looked after her neighbour's child when they had a crisis and done all her own shopping. He realised that for years he had controlled her life and denied her the opportunity of taking responsibility for herself. By being overprotective he had slowed down her spiritual growth.

When we take responsibility for someone else's decisions we do not serve their highest growth.

Eileen had a twelve-year-old son. He kept plaguing her to let him stay with some friends of his. She was not happy about this and whenever he asked the dreaded question, 'Please can I stay with Bill and Jo tonight,' an argument would ensue. He knew that she did not like him to stay at Bill and Jo's house but kept asking all the same.

One day she decided to change her response. She said, 'Don't ask me for permission to do something you know I don't like. If you want to stay there you take the decision and the responsibility for it.' Her son was horrified. He did not particularly like staying with Bill and Jo but liked to blame his mother for saying 'No'. Now he had to take responsibility himself. He didn't ask again. He didn't stay with them again. The arguments stopped.

We disempower children by taking responsibility for them. A disempowered person is always angry.

A friend of mine was running workshops to help parents of the children in a local school. Her opening words were, 'If you are having problems with your child, do not expect him to change. Change your own behaviour and your child will follow suit.'

The parents were stunned but saw the logic of it. The biggest concern of most of the parents was getting their children to do their homework. The parental behaviour included threats, bribes, bullying and doing it for them. In other words parents were taking responsibility for the child doing his homework.

My friend told them, 'Your child is responsible for doing his own homework. If he refuses to do it, just say, "That's fine. Don't do it then." However, do not sign the child's card. Let him face the consequences himself.'

The parents looked dazed and totally relieved. The teachers backed my friend up and the children started to do their homework voluntarily.

True responsibility is the ability to respond to the needs of all around you — to flowers, trees, animals, humans and the planet. An evolved being responds graciously to every living creature in the Universe.

I had lunch with a lady who I admire very much. She is a healer who runs groups and a healing centre and has helped many thousands of people. She always seems pleasant and calm and radiant. I asked how her pathway started and she told me that her father was schizophrenic. He behaved in a bizarre way and was a dangerous parent to have. She did not blame him or feel angry. She accepted that she had chosen him as a parent to teach her incredible lessons. She said that she had learnt so much as a result of her experiences with him that she wanted to help others. The challenges of her early life gave her compassion and strength which prepared her for the responsibility of the healing centre.

It is very common for a child to carry the beliefs dumped on them by their parents. Sometimes we take on board a projection from a teacher.

A young man called James had always felt inadequate. Then he realised that when he was ten years old he had felt below par because of problems at home. At that time his teacher had constantly reiterated to him 'You're stupid'. He had taken it in. It had become one of his programmes and he had been carrying the burden ever since.

It was time to return the belief to its source. He sat down, and visualised that teacher, Mrs. B, coming to him. He handed the belief back to her. Only then was he able to remember times when he had been bright, alert and praised for his quickness. His sense of self-esteem and worth blossomed.

If you are carrying a family belief, a family emotion, a family secret, hand it back to the person who gave it to you. Do it lovingly but firmly.

Alternatively, call in the angels and ascended masters and ask them to transmute the energy.

> *When we carry other people's burdens we stop them from growing and taking mastery of their own life. We hold back their evolution and that of the planet. If you take responsibility for someone else's feelings you dishonour them.*

If you cannot tell someone about a situation or how you feel in case they feel hurt, angry, jealous or depressed, you are taking responsibility for their feelings. You do them an injustice. When you speak honestly about your own feelings you are taking responsibility for yourself and in doing so you release the other person as well as yourself.

Most of us project our own feelings on to others. In other words, we know we would be angry in that situation so we imagine they would be angry too. We dump our stuff on to them.

If you say, 'I can't tell Joan because I know she will be so jealous,' you are projecting your jealousy on to her. Joan may well be jealous but if she is, it is her own responsibility.

When we understand the spiritual Law of Responsibility, we no longer blame anybody else or project our feelings on to others. However, we do take total responsibility for every single thing that happens in our life, for every feeling that we have, every emotion and every thought.

A master asks the question, 'How did I make this happen? What thought or feelings did I send out? What actions have I taken in the past to create this?' and, most important of all, 'How can I change things?'

> *When you take responsibility for your life you become a master.*

 I am responsible for myself and my own pathways and allow others to be responsible for theirs.

CHAPTER TWENTY-ONE

THE LAW OF DISCRIMINATION

A baby is not expected to know the difference between right and wrong. An adult is. The more evolved we are the more we are expected to discriminate. Naturally we are tested. If you are told something, given guidance, meet a person, are offered a job, check internally whether or not it feels right to you.

Many years ago when my children were in their teens I took them away for a short holiday. We visited a market where a glib salesman was selling special puffer thermos flasks. My daughter, Lauren, decided I needed one. She argued that they were very cheap and I would always regret it if I did not take advantage of the opportunity. Despite my misgivings I bought one. When we tested it at home it leaked like a sieve. Lauren laughed her head off and said, 'What do you expect if you buy cheap stuff from the market?' We had a good laugh but I now see what a wonderful lesson in discrimination it was. I allowed a fifteen-year-old to persuade me against my better judgment and I bore the consequences.

I read in the newspaper about a man who had embezzled money from many of his clients. Afterwards there was a general consensus that there was something funny about him and they had never really trusted him. They did not listen to their intuition. They did not discern. Sometimes the consequences of non-discrimination are very severe.

Some time ago I received a very sad letter from a woman

who had attended one of my angel workshops. In all my workshops we ask for spiritual protection and connect with only the highest and purest beings. I remind participants that angels of light make you feel warm, peaceful and loved.

In her letter she told me that all her life she had been very afraid and unhappy. At the workshop she met her guardian angel and learnt to communicate with him. She was filled with a sense of peace, serenity and happiness. Life took on new meaning for her as she sensed her beautiful angel around her and felt his love and protection. Three months later she read in a book that it was dangerous to connect with angels as they might be dark angels. All her peace, happiness and serenity fell away and a sense of desolation and fear enveloped her. She wrote to me to ask what she could do as she was now too frightened to connect with her guardian angel again.

When we work with the invisible forces we must always use discrimination. If any impressions do not feel right to you, ignore them and close down. If you sense that you are connecting to a high and loving presence, enjoy it and follow the prompting. I could only remind her that feelings of peace, happiness, serenity, purpose and inspiration indicate that we are connecting with angels of light. I hope that by using protection, prayer and discernment she will open up to the presence of her angel again.

Young souls are like travellers exploring every road and path. They need the experiences of different routes, dry, muddy, wide, narrow, light, dark. They travel with everyone and anyone. Older and wiser souls are expected to choose the appropriate route for their purpose and discriminate in their choice of companions.

At a deep level we know everything. Our gut feeling tells

us whether someone is being honest or not. We often disregard this because our logical mind argues against it or because we do not want to believe it. We override our intuition. If we do not discern we bear the resultant karma. Furthermore, another test will come towards us differently disguised.

To discriminate against someone on grounds of sex, colour, religion or size is not spiritual. Many people feel that it is being judgmental to discriminate on any grounds whatsoever. They feel they should accept anyone into their lives or business. This is not so. We are called on to use discernment. Does that person's energy feel right as a friend or a therapist? Do you really sense that your business partner will support your ideas? Is it comfortable to have a date with that person? You have the right to decide who you want in your life. It is not being judgmental to say no. It is discrimination.

If your friends all want to see a violent film, it is time to discern not just whether you want to go with them but if they resonate with you as friends. Are you ready to be different and stand up for what you sense is right for you?

To an ant a piece of paper on a desk may seem like a desert. To a human it may be an important document. To an astronaut, surveying the greater scheme of things, it is insignificant. All are right from their perspective. Writers and teachers all experience a different spiritual perspective. They can only communicate from the level they have reached. They may all be correct from their viewpoint.

However, the dark forces now are using impure channels to bring forward very slightly tainted information. A small distortion of the truth here and there can cause confusion and this is their aim.

A man spoke to me after a workshop. He had been to many spiritual workshops and read dozens of books. He was frantic about the different things he had heard. 'Everyone can't be right,' he said. 'So what should I believe?' His test is to use discernment. I suggested that he sit quietly and listen to his inner voice, then accept what resonated with him.

Do not throw away *everything* because *some* things do not feel right.

No one can know the whole truth while in a body. Only the Creator knows that, but stay open and let your intuition guide you.

*Listen to your intuition and
trust it to guide you.*

CHAPTER TWENTY-TWO

THE LAW OF AFFIRMATION

Affirmations are thoughts or words constantly repeated until they enter the unconscious mind and become part of your programming. They make firm your thoughts and words and have an incredibly powerful effect on you. Most of us affirm unconsciously all the time. We consistently repeat thoughts until we anchor them in our mind. We make the same statements again and again until they become our reality.

Our constantly repeated statements may be positive or negative, wholesome or unwholesome. Your unconscious mind is like a computer. It is impersonal. It accepts all input without discrimination. So your affirmations enter the files of your unconscious mind and profoundly affect how you feel and act.

Imagine a nail being hammered into a piece of wood. Push it in with your thumb and it will take a long time to make an impression. A tap with a hammer pushes it in a little way. Each successive hit embeds it more firmly. Thoughts push the beliefs into your mind. Affirmations hammer them in.

If you constantly think 'I am a failure' you gradually believe you are a failure and then you act it out. You are making an unhelpful affirmation.

I knew a man who incessantly grumbled that his back played him up whenever he wanted to play golf. He was angry with his back and brooded about it. When I suggested that his negative affirmations were not serving him, he looked at me darkly and said, 'You don't understand. That's how it is.' Then he added loudly and emphatically, 'My back always plays me up when I want to play golf.' He affirmed his way to his painful reality.

The more energy and emphasis we put into our affirmations the more deeply they enter our belief system.

If you constantly repeat that you always have miserable holidays, you bring it about in three ways.

You selectively remember bad times.

You act in ways that cause you misery.

The Universe brings to you what you believe, in this case misery.

The Universe literally rearranges itself to give you what you believe.

The Law of Affirmation states that you bring about what you affirm. Affirm that you are what you want to be. You will become it sooner than you think.

Affirm that you have what you want to have and it will magnetise towards you.

To make affirmations, speak your words with energy and intent.

This will hammer them into your mind more powerfully.

Make sure your affirmations contain only positive words.

The unconscious mind cannot compute negatives. It

simply ignores them. For example, 'I don't want to live in this house,' constantly affirmed, enters the unconscious mind without the 'don't' as 'I want to live in this house'. An appropriate affirmation would be, 'I am ready to move house.' It is even more effective to describe the house you wish to move to in detail and affirm, 'I am happy and fulfilled in my new home.'

I talked to a lady who had been through a difficult period in life. She came from a background where a stiff upper lip was valued and did not want to show her feelings. She told me that she kept repeating to herself, 'I refuse to be unhappy.' Of course this entered her unconscious mind as a constant message of 'unhappy, unhappy, unhappy'. She was trying to fight misery while affirming it.

'I am not going to lose' enters the mind's computer as 'lose, lose, lose' because the 'not' is ignored. Use only the positive: 'I am a winner.'

Affirmations must be in the present tense.

A computer has no concept of past or future. If you affirm that you are going to be healthy tomorrow, tomorrow never comes. Affirm 'I am healthy now'. You become what you affirm. The quickest way to have a beautiful garden is to affirm your garden is beautiful now. It helps you to hold the vision and bring it about.

Effective affirmations are simple.

Complicated affirmations are so confusing that they alert

the conscious mind to try to understand them. I have seen unhelpful affirmations like this one: 'I am no longer afraid of having a relationship because I love my father and forgive all he did to me when I was a child, so I deserve to have a good partner now who loves me and is interested in the same things as I am.' It is better to make two simple affirmations. 'I love my father. I deserve a happy relationship.' When those affirmations have taken root, affirm, 'I have a happy relationship now.' Then visualise constantly that you have a happy relationship and act as if you are contented and deserving.

Affirmations which are rhyming or rhythmic slip into your unconscious mind easily.

A man who had been under the weather for some time started to affirm, 'I am healthy and strong all day long.' He said he found himself standing taller and breathing more deeply. Not only did he feel healthier but he also felt more confident. Affirmations have a ripple effect which improves other areas of your life.

If you are having a difficult day hum these words to yourself. 'I am happy and bright. Everything is going right.' Watch your day change.

There is a whole chapter of rhyming affirmations in my book *A Time for Transformation*. One of my favourites is 'Calm and centred, quiet and still. I love myself and always will.' I find it soothes me and reminds me to honour my worth.

You can open your mind to receive affirmations more easily if you are in a trance. For instance, if you are daydreaming your unconscious mind is open to receiving affirmations. If your conscious mind is fully engaged, as when you are watching television or focused on work, entry to your unconscious mind is easier. If you are deeply relaxed or dozing, or even in a light sleep, affirmations slip in readily. You can use these natural trance states to enhance and speed up the absorption of affirmations. One way is to play affirmative tapes or record a tape of the affirmations you need.

It is easy during a natural trance to take on the affirmations other people make for you. Imagine this. A little boy is daydreaming or deeply entranced watching a caterpillar crawling along a leaf. His mother says angrily, 'Hurry up. You're so slow.' If said often enough or with enough vehemence this can easily slip into the child's mind and become a belief that he is slow. He has allowed someone else to programme his unconscious.

We set up problems for ourselves without realising what we are doing. If your partner is in his study deeply absorbed in work and you shout up the stairs, 'Don't forget the dinner party,' his unconscious mind has ignored 'don't'. He has absorbed, 'Forget the dinner party.' You think all is well because he has probably replied, 'OK.' However, it was his unconscious mind that automatically responded. Consciously your words may not have registered. We do not always realise when someone is abstracted or in a natural trance, so get into the habit of making positive statements such as 'Remember the dinner party'.

A good hypnotherapist will use a variety of techniques, including simple relaxation and visualisation, to induce a client into a trance. One purpose of this is to allow positive affirmations to enter and take deep root in the client's unconscious mind while he is aware and co-operating with the suggestions. This can be a powerful and life-changing use of affirmations.

Affirmations need to be constantly repeated.

When you choose an affirmation repeat it whenever you have a free moment, driving the car, walking, in the loo, swimming. Fill your mind with your positive statements and you will soon notice the difference in your life.

Constantly make positive affirmations to others. By repeatedly telling your little girl she is capable you will help her to become capable.

Affirm to your children, your family and your friends that they are clever and how much you love them. Constantly remind them of their good points and you will be raising the vibrations and confidence of those around you.

Examples of affirmations are:

I am healthy and happy.

Everyone loves me.

I have a satisfying, well-paid job as an office manager.

I am an ascended master of great love and light.

I am an ascended being of infinite patience and wisdom.

My life is full of joy and laughter.

Remember to affirm what you want to be as if you are already there. This is a quick route to where you want to be. Then act as if it has already become your reality.

THE LAW
OF
AFFIRMATION

Constantly affirm you are
who you want to be and
you will soon become it.

CHAPTER TWENTY-THREE

THE LAW OF PRAYER

Prayer is communicating with God. Whether we realise it or not, God is on the other end of the phone line, listening to us all the time. Every word and every thought we send along it is a prayer.

Worry is negative prayer. It is telling God how frightened you are. It also reinforces all the things that you don't want to happen. Edgar Cayce said, 'Why worry when you can pray?' meaning that we must direct our thoughts to Source in a positive, focused way.

The way you pray is important. Imagine you are a rich, powerful, omniscient king. Moreover, you have the highest interest of your people at heart. Every day there is a long line of supplicants wanting to talk to you.

There is the beggar, who whines and grovels, desperately abasing himself for money. He is an eternal victim and you know that if you grant his wish, he will spend it unwisely and tomorrow will be begging again.

The bargainer says, 'If you'll grant me this, I will work for you.' As an omniscient king you read his heart so he cannot fool you.

Then the manipulators come up to you shaking their fists. 'I'll be angry with you if you don't give me a job.' 'If you don't help me I'll kill myself.' 'If you don't give me a break I'll give up completely, so there.' From your detached position on your throne are you likely to grant these requests?

Your next supplicant is a trickster. He's shooting a line

with a 'Let's see what I can get' attitude. He thinks a petition is worth a try but he has no intention of changing his way of life. Sorry, lad.

Following him comes a sad woman with a droopy face. 'I don't deserve anything. I'm a miserable sinner but please give it to me anyway.' You know that her pitifully low levels of self-worth and deservingness will ensure that she will soon lose what you give her.

The greedy person follows her. 'I want more, more, more.'

At last there is the person who looks you in the eye and says, 'This is what I want to achieve. These are the plans I have already set into action. This is what I need from you.' You get off your throne and become a fully supporting partner.

Then there is the person who prays from her heart. Her prayers touch your heart. You respond to those prayers.

Another prays with purity of intention. These you grant.

So God does answer all prayers. Sometimes, mercifully for us, He says 'No'. Thankfully we do not get everything we pray for.

The Creator also answers prayers in a practical sort of way rather than with miracles. There is a well-known story about a devout man who was convinced that God would always save and protect him. One winter there were terrible storms in the area where he lived. The rain lashed unceasingly. When the downstairs of his house was flooded he moved upstairs. A boat passed by and the rescuers called out to him to get into it but he replied, 'No, God will save me.' The floods grew higher and higher and he climbed on to the roof. A helicopter came by and sent down a rope for him but he refused to accept it. 'No, I don't need it. God will rescue

me.' He drowned and met St Peter at the pearly gates. The
man said petulantly to St Peter, 'Why didn't God save me?'
St Peter replied, 'He sent a boat and a helicopter. What more
did you want?' So look to the obvious and practical things in
your life as the answers to your prayers.

The Law of Prayer is – ask, believing, and it is granted.
Faith is an active ingredient in bringing your prayers about.

The moment you have offered your prayer, start thanking
God for it. Then prepare to receive what you have asked for.
So, if you have ordered ten fruit trees from the warehouse in
the Heavens, say thanks and then go and dig your ground,
prepare the holes, buy in the right fertilisers and be ready for
the fruit trees to come. Your faith will precipitate the arrival
of the trees.

Many people pray without really expecting the prayer to
be granted, so they take no action. What they do not realise
is that faith activates a response from the Universe.

I had lunch with a friend whose husband had just had
a heart attack. As he recovered he said to her that he had
always wanted to visit Australia and he really regretted that
he had never been there. They did not have enough money so
they prayed and thanked God for the money for him to go to
Australia, knowing that God wanted him to have his heart's
desire. He phoned the travel agent and booked a ticket which
had to be paid for within a few days. Next day a credit card,
which they had not applied for, flopped through the door and
he bought the ticket on it, knowing he could pay it back over
the next year. She laughed as she said, 'Next time I'll pray
for the money to come in a way which doesn't have to be
paid back!'

When you ask for one or more people to pray with

you and hold your vision, it strengthens the power of the prayer. A client asked me to pray for his son, who was failing academically at school and being very disruptive. Six months later he wrote to me to thank me for my prayers. He said that an amazing change had come over his son who was now top of the class. He was also on the football team and his teacher had said that he was a pleasure to have in the form. My client also prayed daily for his son, while I was the anchor who held faith. It is a very powerful combination.

Love wants you to have your heart's desire. Love does not want his beloved to suffer. God is love. The block to receiving is at your end.

Many people pray for something but are then not prepared to receive what they asked for. I know someone who asked for a car. A little while later an elderly aunt offered him her car and he was horrified. 'I can't accept your car,' he told her. It was only later that he realised that God was answering his prayer through his aunt.

People sometimes say to me that they have been praying for something for years but nothing happens. If it is a prayer for the collective, such as world peace or healing the ozone layer, your prayers are part of a continuous stream going to the Godhead and can be continued.

However, if you are praying for something personal, there is a time to let go. Imagine a little girl asking her dad to mend her doll. Every day she goes to him with her doll and asks him to look at it but she refuses to let it go. She will not hand it over to be examined and mended. Clearly he cannot do anything about it until she is prepared to release it.

Say your prayer for a month or for however long it feels right and then stop for a while. It may come to you to change your prayer in some way. This is an indication that things have moved on for you.

Asking for something bad to happen to someone else or asking for victory over someone else is a mockery of prayer. The negative energy eventually boomerangs back to hit the sender.

When you offer a prayer, keep holding the vision of perfection. If you pray for peace, picture and feel peace coming about. If you pray for healing for someone, picture that person healthy and strong. But remember that death too is a healing. Always pray for the highest good to happen. The divine perspective is greater than yours.

Long complicated prayers or prayers by rote are not real prayers. They are often words to impress others. Prayer is simple, sincere, authentic and from the heart.

Pray from a calm, centred space. People often write me anguished letters telling how they desperately plead for help. It is very hard for the angels to get through a disturbed aura to give such help. So relax. Make your aura gold. Ask quietly and miracles tend to happen.

This is how to activate the Law of Prayer.

First ask.

Then detach from the result.

Thank God for responding.

Hold your faith.

Prepare for it to be granted.

Here is a well-known anonymous poem which sums up the efficacy of prayer.

PRAYER

I got up early one morning
And rushed right into the day;
I had so much to accomplish
That I didn't have time to pray.

Problems just tumbled about me,
And heavier came each task.
'Why doesn't God help me?' I wondered.
He answered, 'You didn't ask.'

I wanted to see joy and beauty,
But the day toiled on, grey and bleak,
I wondered why God didn't show me,
He said, 'But you didn't seek.'

I tried to come into God's presence;
I used all my keys at the lock.
God gently and lovingly chided,
'My child, you didn't knock.'

I woke up early this morning,
And paused before entering the day,
I had so much to accomplish
That I had to take time to pray.

*When you pray you are moving towards God and God is
moving twice as fast towards you.*

Ask, believing, and it is
already granted.

CHAPTER TWENTY-FOUR

THE LAW OF MEDITATION

Meditation is listening to the voice of God. It necessitates placing yourself away from the hustle and bustle of life in order to hear the still quiet voice of the Divine.

Have you ever spoken on the phone to one of those people who constantly talks at you, without listening to your replies? Every time you try to get a word in edgeways the other person ignores it and chats on. When I am trying to communicate with such a person I disconnect as soon as I can. As above so below. The Universe will metaphorically put the receiver down if you do not listen to its replies.

If you constantly pray without taking time to listen to the reply, you get no response because your mind-chatter won't let God get a word in edgeways. Most of us have monkey minds, in other words eternally chattering thoughts. The aim and intention of meditation is to still the chatter long enough for Source to drop in His seeds of guidance and wisdom. During these still quiet moments we are open to inspiration and answers to our questions. Sometimes we receive a divine response immediately. More often we feel a sense of quiet and stillness, while the seeds are planted. They sprout and grow over time and become evident later in our lives.

I was discussing the power of meditation with a friend the other day. She told me that a friend of hers had recently taken part in an all-night chanting meditation. This friend had just bought and decorated a one-bedroom flat. As she drove home after the meditation she felt light and clear. Suddenly she had a revelation that she must start teaching classes and would need a house with a large room in which to do this. She took a detour from her normal route and this took her past an old house with a 'For sale' sign in the garden. She knew it was her house. When she went to view it, it had a forty-foot sitting room. Because of the work she had put into her tiny flat, she made a profit on it and was able to put down a deposit on the house. Within weeks she was in her new home and her classes had started. She knew that the night of meditation had enabled the Divine to drop in the seed-thought of a totally unexpected new life for her.

'Look within and the kingdom of heaven is yours.' During meditation, we have an opportunity to explore the resources available to us. It is here that we find our true selves. We live in hell or heaven according to our inner world. Meditation allows our divine self to expand so that we free ourselves from hell and create heaven.

There are many people who cannot bear to meditate formally. Their quiet, still moments come when they tend the garden or walk in nature. Creative times, such as when you are painting, playing music or doing pottery, silence the mind-chatter and open the right brain to receive divine inspiration. Anything that empties the mind for a moment allows you to slip through the gap into the divine energy. That is the purpose of meditation.

There are many formal ways of meditating. All require the same basic preparation.

Find a time when you can be undisturbed and at peace.

Wear loose, comfortable clothing.

Sit cross-legged or on a chair.

MEDITATION

Keep your back straight.
Relax.
These are some of the most popular types of meditation:

1. Stare at a candle until your eyelids feel heavy.
   After you close them continue to watch the candle
   flame in your mind's eye.
   Focus on it intently.
   When your mind is still let it go.

2. Focus on your breath as it enters and leaves
   your nostrils.
   Count from 1 to 5 on the in-breath.
   Count from 1 to 5 on the out-breath.
   When your mind is still let it go.

3. Silently repeat a mantra or the divine names or
   chant a mantra aloud.
   Mantras and names of gods are sacred words which
   call in divine attributes.
   Many people prefer to use their own personal
   mantra which has been given to them by a spiritual
   teacher who they trust.
   When your mind is still let it go.

Power-filled mantras are:
   Om nama shivaya.
   Om mani padme hum.
   Jesus Christ.
   Om Sai Ram for followers of Sai Baba.
   Kodoish, kodoish, kodoish, Adonai T'sbayoth.

THE LAWS
OF
HIGHER AWARENESS

As with any spiritual practice, a regular routine of meditating at a certain time and place each day is a great help. If you can create an altar on which you place a candle, crystals, photos of saints and masters and items that are sacred to you, that really raises the vibrations. It also helps to burn joss sticks or incense. Before you start you may like to play sacred music and offer a prayer. Call in the Great Beings of Light to be with you during your meditation.

When I was staying in India at the ashram of Amma, the hugging Mother, I heard a wonderful story which puts another perspective on meditation. One of her swamis was giving a discourse. A swami is one who has taken a vow of poverty, chastity and obedience and is in service to their guru. This particular swami was incredibly handsome with twinkling brown eyes, a deep chocolate brown voice and wonderful laugh. One of his tasks was to lead the nightly meditation in the temple. In his rich voice he would lead three chants of *Ma Ohm*. He did it with great reverence and you could hear a pin drop amongst the thousands of worshippers. He clearly loved doing it.

He told us this story. One day, when the temple was packed, as usual he waited for total silence before he started. They all chanted the beautiful *Ma Ohm*. It was tailing into awesome silence when a small child sang out in a high squeaky voice, '*Ohhhhm.*' Everyone tittered and he was furious.

Gathering his composure he intoned the second *Ma Ohm*. Again the child broke the silence with '*Ohhhhm*' and everyone in the temple roared with laughter. He was livid. The child was spoiling his precious meditation.

There was nothing for it but to chant the third *Ma Ohm* with as much composure as he could muster. At the end of it the irrepressible child giggled loudly and everyone collapsed with laughter.

He was so angry about this horrible brat who had ruined his meditation that he planned to tell Amma that he thought children should be banned from the temple during the meditation.

He strode up to see her as soon as he could. 'Amma, about that child,' he blustered.

'Yes,' she said softly, 'Wasn't it lovely.'

'Lovely! What do you mean lovely?' he spluttered. 'That child spoilt my meditation.'

Amma looked at him gently. 'I think you've got it wrong,' she told him. 'Meditation is not about being heavy and serious. It is about bliss and the child brought in the pure bliss of innocence.'

Meditation is the doorway to bliss.

In the silence you will receive pearls of divine wisdom.

CHAPTER TWENTY-FIVE

THE LAW OF CHALLENGE

*The spiritual Law of Challenge states that if you challenge
a disembodied entity three times in the name of God, it must
reveal its true identity or disappear.*

If you wish to be awake by a certain time you set your
alarm clock before you go to sleep. Some people wake
naturally just before this time. Others have to be jangled
or shaken out of sleep. Others keep turning over and going
back to sleep.

You are here on Earth on a spiritual quest. You would
not be happy if you missed the opportunity to partake in
your quest because you were asleep.

It may be that you became aware of your spiritual destiny
gently and easily. However, many do not. Before you came
into the oblivion of life in a body your soul set an alarm
just in case you did not wake up in time to do the work
you came to do. If you were still asleep your call might have
been something that shook you to the depth of your being.

The reason wake-up calls can be so painful is because it
takes a trauma to open some people to full spiritual awareness.
Alarms are going off right now for people all over the globe,
alerting them to the world beyond the physical.

Personal development and self-awareness courses open
people up gently. As the spiritual self lights up there is often an
awakening of psychic abilities. In many the third-eye centre is
unfurling its petals, revealing clairvoyance or deep intuition.

CHALLENGE

In this plane of duality there is darkness and light. For everything in the light, there is its counterpart in the dark.

If you are asleep in a darkened room you do not notice moths and they are unaware of you. When you switch on the light the moths will gravitate towards it. As a person wakes to his spiritual self, his light becomes stronger and can be seen. Then dark beings, those of less than pure intentions, are attracted towards the radiant soul. Just as moths are attracted to the light, so are the darker entities attracted to your spiritual light.

When the light is really bright and the moth black, it is obvious what it is. But if the light is dim for any reason or the moth pale, it is not always easy to see. Your task is to discern between good and bad, challenge if in doubt, and to make your light so strong that the darkness cannot affect you. You merely show it up for what it is. Usually your own powers of discernment will tell you if a 'voice' or an entity feels good or bad. If in doubt, challenge.

As above so below. If a stranger came up to you and asked you to lend him money, you would probably look into his eyes and directly ask whatever questions you needed answers to. The eyes are the windows of the soul. You would look in and sense whether the person was being true and honest. That might be enough.

However, if you were in any doubt you would check him out.

If he said that he had direct connections with an influential lord you might well be wary. On the other hand, if you knew someone well and trusted him, you would accept his word.

The genuine meter reader or policeman is pleased when you ask for proof of identity before you let him into your home. It cuts out fraud and safeguards the reputation of the profession. Only the bogus person is bothered if you challenge him. Similarly, Higher Beings who approach you and want to work with you are pleased if you challenge. It means you are being careful and are practising discernment. It shows them that you are responsible.

If a being approaches you in a dream, meditation or psychic visitation asking you to do something, listen to your intuition. Then if you are in any doubt whatsoever, ask it to state its purpose in approaching you. If it gives you a message that confuses you, be careful. If you have been working with your guides and angels for some time and recognise their energy and trust them, you do not need to challenge. They are friends.

You might challenge like this. 'In the name of God and all that is light, who are you and what is your intention in approaching me?' This must be repeated three times and an answer will be received, possibly in the form of a strong thought directly into the mind, an impression or a sensation.

If the being has declared itself by name your challenge might be, 'In the name of Christ, are you a being of the highest and purest light?' It is insufficient to challenge with words such as 'Are you of the light?' because this can mean just about anything. A playful child with a torch is a light but I would not want it to guide me. Your deceased alcoholic uncle may be trying to get hold of you but if you did not trust him in life there is no reason to rely on him just because he is in spirit.

There are many levels of light, from tricksters to great and wonderful masters.

The spiritual Law of Challenge is for your protection.

THE LAW
OF
CHALLENGE

If in doubt challenge those who wish to enter your space.

THE
LAWS OF
HIGHER
FREQUENCY

CHAPTER TWENTY-SIX

THE LAW OF FREQUENCY OR VIBRATION

Fear is a heavy vibration (low frequency). Calmness, peace and love are light ones (high frequency). Humour dissolves difficult situations and lifts the energy. Love heals the treacle of grief. High, light vibrations dissolve and transmute low, heavy ones. While panic rampages like wildfire if unchecked, the presence of one calm person douses the flames and soothes everyone's fears.

Janey came to see me because she absolutely dreaded visiting her in-laws. Christmas was coming and she feared that it would be the usual very difficult heavy time. She informed me that her father-in-law was fat and pompous, her mother-in-law was plump and plaintive, while her husband's brother and sister were seriously boring people. I suggested that in order to lighten the vibration she picture them as animals. Her face lit up immediately and she said that her father-in-law was a penguin, her mother-in-law a cow, her brother-in-law a horse and her sister-in-law a sheep.

Christmas Day arrived and she sat at the festive table with the penguin, the cow, the horse and the sheep around her. Bubbles of laughter rose up in her as she watched the interaction between the animals. In her imagination she saw the penguin shovelling a fish into his mouth. She heard the cow mooing to the bleating sheep. She couldn't stop herself laughing. Her laughter was infectious and soon everyone was giggling without quite knowing why. It was the best Christmas she had ever had. Afterwards the family said what a real pleasure it had been to see her looking so happy. Her lightness had changed their attitude.

Angels have a wonderful sense of humour and love the vibration of laughter. They take themselves lightly and their presence makes you feel lighter.

I was told this story by Mhairi Kent. Many years ago she and her husband had just moved house. They were not getting on and their small son was very sickly and asthmatic. She was desperately tired and felt she could not go on any longer. It was a bitterly cold November night and she went to Hammersmith bridge, intending to jump off the bridge. It was 2 a.m. and there was no one about. She thought, 'The tide is probably right now.' She had deliberately chosen her nice camel coat because it was heavy. Clutching her handbag and expensive coat, she contemplated the water below and prepared to jump.

Suddenly she was aware of a tramp who sidled up to her and said, 'Excuse me, Miss. Are you going to jump? If you're going to jump could I have your coat?' Then his eyes moved to her handbag and he said, 'What's in your handbag? You're not going to need that, are you?' Suddenly she found herself laughing. She laughed for about forty seconds. Then she looked and he was gone. She ran to both ends of the bridge but there was no one there. He had disappeared.

Her sense of humour had returned and it broke the dark energy within her. She went home and started a new life. She believed he was an angel who had appeared as a tramp in her time of need.

Cynical or critical people send out darts of low-frequency

energy. A friend told me that her mother was an intensely critical old woman. Whenever she took her children to visit her they would all be the subjects of her wicked tongue. On the way home they would have a competition to see who had sustained the worst insults. She and the children would laugh hysterically as they discussed the appalling things the old mother had said to them. Laughter was their way of shaking out the barbs.

Anger and rage are low-vibration energies. Underlying them is always fear and a feeling of powerlessness. When we stay calm and centred, we sustain a high vibration. We are empowered. When we hold this energy we can speak our truth. As we calmly express how we feel it dissolves the feelings of anger and rage.

There is a saying that one bad apple infects the whole barrel. Undoubtedly a bad person can corrupt others who are weak but has no impact on strong people.

> *However, a strong person of pure dedicated intention can positively influence bad people.*

Everyone knows that animals respond to frequencies of which we are not aware. A dog will growl if you are frightened of it. A horse will immediately know if you are scared and respond accordingly. Teachers know that if they are nervous or stressed the children in their class will behave abominably. If you are feeling strong, confident and loving all creatures and plants will respond positively to the high frequency you emit.

I was talking to a student teacher who was very distressed because the children had behaved so badly that day and been so angry. We discussed this and I helped her to release her fears. She asked her angel to talk to the angels of every child in the class. Next morning before she went to her school, she asked the angels to work through her. She could not believe it when she walked into the classroom. There sat thirty-four eight-year-olds at their desks, quietly smiling at her like little angels themselves. It was the best lesson she had ever taught.

Angels have a high-frequency vibration. Simply thinking about them raises your consciousness.

To do something because you feel you should or ought to do it has a low vibration. Guilt or obligation are not good reasons for doing things. When you change your attitude or decide to do what you genuinely want to do, you radiate high-frequency energy.

The sooner we do only those things which give us a sense of joy and enthusiasm, the more quickly we will raise our frequency and that of those around us.

Lack of self-worth comes from negative self-talk. It is black imagination and, needless to say, emits a low vibration. On the other hand, self-worth and confidence radiate high-frequency light.

There is a fairy tale about a little duck who felt he was different and ugly. He believed that nobody wanted to be with him. So the little duck isolated himself from his fellow ducklings because he felt so alone. He persuaded himself he was different and undesirable to be with. Then one day an enormous and very beautiful white bird floated regally towards him across the lake. It was a swan, who addressed him in surprise, 'What are you doing here amongst these ducks? You're not a duckling. You are a swan.' From the moment the little cygnet learnt who he really was, he felt transformed. He held his head high. He realised that, as a swan, he really was different and he was proud of it. He knew that he was going to grow up into a beautiful white bird. From that moment he acted as a swan. He radiated confidence and self-worth.

Remember who you truly are. You are an amazing being. You are a beautiful, incredible, vibrant and alive being. When you realise this and act as a master of light you radiate a high vibration.

All you have to do is realise who you are and accept it.

You can use your imagination to breathe confidence, joy or beautiful colours into your aura. You can visualise positive solutions to your challenges. This will raise you into a high-frequency being.

When you live your life with charm, grace, joy, integrity, generosity and any of the other great qualities, you will automatically dissolve the low-frequency emissions of others and raise them to a higher level. Under the Law of Karma, wonderful things will start coming back to you.

Swearing forms a heavy, dark thought-cloud. So do thoughts of violence, hurt, abuse, jealousy, guilt and any other negative emotion. They can be transmuted by forgiveness, compassion and joy. Chanting *om* and other sacred mantras and prayers raises a high-frequency energy. So does saying the names of gods, archangels and masters. Spiritual books, classical music and beautiful paintings raise the vibrations of a room. If enough people focus light into an area of town where there has been darkness and violence, goodness and peace take over.

Illness or disease have a heavy vibration which blocks the flow of vital life-force. Healing takes place when high-frequency energy is channelled to that person. It transmutes the heavy vibration of the illness and allows health to blossom.

Wealth has a vibration. If you wish to be rich think rich.

Success has its own frequency. Seek out and mix with successful people and your vibration will start to match theirs.

If you wish to increase your spiritual light mix with spiritual people so that your vibration and theirs start to merge.

In order to bring love and light into the planet, bring in columns of white light to allow angels and higher beings to enter. With your thoughts, create bridges of light to people and places, so that help and healing may go to them.

Your name has a vibration. When it is spoken it calls in your lessons. Before you were born you telepathically imparted the name you wished to be called to your parents. Many children are called by a nickname or abbreviated form of their name. This is because they cannot cope with all their lessons coming to them at that time. Often when they are older they use their full name. If you change your name, you call in new lessons. If your name is said crossly, especially when you are a child, you get the impression that your lessons are difficult. When it is said lovingly you know that you can handle what is presented to you harmoniously.

These are the lessons you are learning if you have the following vowels in your name:

a   Purification. This is about letting go of angers and

other negative energies or beliefs that you hold.
Release the old.

e   Relationships. You are learning to relate to others
harmoniously and with integrity.

i   Awareness. You are learning to be aware of who
you are and what the world is about.

o   Innocence. You are learning to live in your essence.
This is about living for the now and being yourself.
Express your true self.

u   Boundaries. You are learning to set your boundaries. Know what emotions are yours and what
belongs to others. Do not carry other people's
responsibilities.

Say your name and everyone else's with great love and you
automatically feel and spread love.

Radiate pure energy and
you will transmute
the unhappiness of those
around you.

CHAPTER TWENTY-SEVEN

THE LAW OF MIRACLES

When something happens which is not normally explainable by our physical laws we have to turn to the spiritual laws.

On Earth we are living in a heavy vibration which is subject to the Law of Karma. Occasionally something happens which allows us to slip through the gap into the divine energy. The divine frequency dissolves and transmutes our lower energy and a miracle occurs. As worldwide consciousness rises more and more people are accessing the Divine. Consequently more people are experiencing miracles.

Genuine forgiveness and unconditional love are divine energies which allow miracles to happen.

Some years ago an elderly lady told me that the only present she wanted for Christmas was a phone call from her son. She had not heard from him for five years and his father had died during that period. When she talked about her son she sounded bitter and hurt. She could not say a good word about him. Bitterness, hurt and anger are heavy, repellent energies. It was no wonder her son did not want to contact her. We talked about the situation for some time until she perceived things differently. Then I suggested she wrote down the anger she felt and burn the paper. This she did. Afterwards she sat quietly and thought about all the things she loved about him. Finally she asked her angel to talk to his angel suggesting he phone at Christmas. He phoned on Christmas Day.

If someone changes their attitude to you completely after

many years, it is a miracle. Anne told me this story. She and her mother had never really got on, partly because her brother was the favourite. It was a terrible shock to the whole family when he committed suicide. Her mother was devastated. She would not talk about it and lived behind an impregnable emotional wall. Her mother talked non-stop and Anne simply could not get through to her.

Anne read my first book *Light Up Your Life* and thought, 'No. It is ridiculous. It is impossible to change so easily. It might work for other people but not for me. I'll never be able to heal the relationship with my mother.'

However, one day she was sitting with her mother, who as usual never for one moment stopped talking. Anne remembered what she had read. She decided to try it. She pictured all her own defences coming down and then her mother's. Then she sat projecting love on to her mother. A few minutes later her mother stopped talking abruptly. She looked at Anne and said, 'There must be another way.' Suddenly she started sharing how she felt when her son died. She told Anne that she and her husband never made love again after that. She became vulnerable and gentle. From that moment Anne and her mother became incredibly close. When she died she felt that she really loved her. Miracles are a natural result of the activation of higher energies.

When we ask the angels or ascended masters or any being from the spiritual hierarchy of light to help us we draw in the divine frequency which transcends physical laws.

An Indian lady shared this story during a workshop. She did a lot of sewing. One day the bobbin of her sewing machine stuck. She could not move it. She did not drive and couldn't carry the heavy machine to the repair shop, so she put it away, hoping for the best. Two days later her husband came home with a pair of trousers he had bought. They were too large and needed taking in. He wanted them for work the next day. She got out the machine and the bobbin was absolutely jammed solid. She tried everything she could to move it but it was stuck fast. Finally she sat quietly and asked the angels to help her. She said, 'My husband needs these trousers tomorrow. Please help.' She went back to the machine and the bobbin moved perfectly.

A close friend of mine was moving house. She had a large sofa of which she was particularly fond. The removal men failed to get it through the front door. They took down part of her neighbour's fence and carried the sofa round to the back of the house. It would not go through the door. They tried every angle for twenty-five minutes. Then my friend quietly asked the angels to take over. Within a minute of asking for help, the sofa was through the door and gracing the sitting room. The removal men were amazed.

I was doing a phone-in on the radio when a lady phoned in with this story. She said that when her dad died she didn't know how she was going to cope with the funeral. She felt so devastated. She could not face it. She was so desperate that she asked for help. In the night an angel came into her dream. She heard hymns being sung around her and felt total peace of mind. This feeling stayed with her and took her through the funeral. She then went on to say that the fountain in her garden pond stopped one day. Friends tried to repair it but could not get it right. She thought the fish would die. Over many days different people tried to mend it. Nothing worked. Before she went to sleep she asked the angels to help with the fountain. In the morning she woke to the sound of water flowing. It was working again.

I was really impressed by a story told by someone during a workshop. She explained that her husband was a businessman who made frequent trips to Germany. During one trip he had stayed the night in a hotel where he regularly stayed. In the morning he got into his car and drove away. To his horror he found himself driving the wrong way down the slip road on to the autobahn towards the oncoming cars. It was a nightmare moment. In panic he called to the angels for help. The next moment he was on the other carriageway in the outside lane driving in the stream of traffic. He simply could not find an explanation for this.

Great beings such as Sai Baba manifest sacred ash, called *vibhutti* ash, from their hands. It is healing ash. There are many stories of *vibhutti* ash forming on pictures of Sai Baba. In the home of a devotee I saw *vibhutti* ash filling the space inside the picture frames. It even came out of the wallpaper in their shrine room and was quite astonishing.

Synchronicities and coincidences are a form of miracle. Spiritual forces are working behind the scenes to co-ordinate the vast and marvellous Universe to make sure that predestined meetings take place.

It can be as simple as my father meeting an Indian on a train and saying to him, 'When I lived in India I was very friendly with a young man. I don't suppose you know him?' It transpired it was this man's first cousin. Of all the tens of millions of people who live in India! It prompted my father to write to his friend again and they stayed in touch. As a result my daughter and I stayed with the family in Delhi over fifty years after my parents knew them. They took us to see all my childhood haunts and we had a marvellous time together.

Coincidences and synchronicities are directed by God and orchestrated by your guides and angels so that you have the opportunity of fulfilling your destiny.

As your vibrations rise you attract more spiritual help, so miracles, synchronicities and coincidences are signals from the Universe that you are on your true pathway.

 Miracles are signs that you are on your true path.

CHAPTER TWENTY-EIGHT

THE LAW OF HEALING

Everything is light. Light is energy. Your physical body is built by the energy of your consciousness. Obviously this is not just by your consciousness in this lifetime. If each soul had only one life on Earth it would be manifestly unjust for one person to be handicapped or ill while another was very healthy. Your body is built by the consciousness of your soul over many lifetimes. All is spiritually perfect. You are here to experience life in a human body. Certain physical choices are made by your soul before birth and may appear as physical limitations. Your personality or lower self makes other choices moment by moment.

There are only two basic emotions on Earth. One is fear and the other is love.

When you resist your chosen experiences through fear, you create blocks in your mental, emotional or spiritual bodies. This eventually causes physical disease.

Inflexible, crystallised beliefs and mental attitudes cause tension. If you hold an organ in tension long enough something physical manifests.

Denied or suppressed emotions sit within the body until they express themselves as physical illness.

When you refuse to acknowledge your spiritual self and your own magnificence you cut off the supply of divine energy and your physical body withers.

All ill health is caused by stuck energy. Where you are happy and flowing with love the cells in your body respond by being healthy.

Your body is like a river of energy, which flows unless
it is silted up. Love is a high-frequency energy which keeps
your body clear and flowing. All manifestations of fear, such as
unexpressed grief, hurt, anger or jealousy are of a low vibration
and are like silt, which blocks the flow. If you open the sluice
gates and send a rush of water down the river, it clears the silt
and washes it out into the ocean. That is the effect of a flow
of healing energy.

*Healing takes place when high-frequency energy flows
through the body, transmuting the stuck energy which caused
the disease.*

As one of the basic laws of the Universe is that you must
ask permission before you interfere with anyone's energy, it is
inappropriate to rush in and give someone healing unless they
agree. There are several reasons for this.

Entering someone's energy system is like entering their home.
It is a private place and you expect to knock before going in.

The illness may be serving them in some way even though
they grumble about it.

The illness is their karma and if they have not learnt the
lesson it offers, you would not be serving their growth by
healing it.

It may not be the right time for them to heal, and their
soul will know this.

They may have a spiritual contract for someone else to
heal them.

If you desire someone else to get better, you are attached
in some way. Cut the cords and allow them to make free
decisions.

It is not up to you to decide what is for the other person's highest good.

When it is impossible to ask if you may give healing, for instance because the other person is too young or too ill, tune in to their Higher Self. When you mentally ask their Higher Self for permission you will receive a distinct impression of an affirmative answer if it is appropriate. If you do not receive this, do not send healing.

Healing is a very powerful frequency. If you insist on imposing it on someone and their karmic illness is taken from them, you must bear it instead in this life or another.

However, be spontaneous. Listen to your intuition. If you come across an accident in which someone is injured, do not hesitate. Go and help. Healing will flow through you automatically if it is right.

It is always appropriate to send light or love or ask the angels to enfold someone.

Healing takes place when someone intercedes by channeling high-frequency energy through the client or if they stimulate the patient's own self-healing mechanisms. Because high vibrations consume lower vibrations healing can also take place when someone has raised a high energy, for instance by dancing or ritual, or by using their own magnetism.

There are many forms of healing.

Spiritual healing. When people dedicate themselves as healers, they attune themselves to the Divine, through spiritual practice, personal development and right living. This allows them to channel high-frequency energy, which flows through the cells of a person's body. When a healer is a clear channel miracles can take place and the soul of the person receiving will use the healing where it needs it most. This may not necessarily be to release the physical. He may accept more patience to cope with his illness. He may feel happier or calmer. He may be freed to pass over. A healing always takes place at some level.

Faith healing. Again the healer channels from the Divine but the healing energy is activated by the power of prayer and faith.

Attitudinal healing. The healer helps his client to change his attitude. When the sick person genuinely forgives himself and the person who has caused the ill feelings of resentment, hate, fear or other stuck emotion, the energy block dissolves and light and love flow again.

Absent healing. Through prayer, spiritual healing or intention light may be sent to someone to heal them.

Magnetic healing. If someone has spare personal energy this may be used to transmute the lower frequencies which block someone else. Energy can be raised by dance or chanting or ritual. Because this is not divine energy the healing may not last unless it triggers the person's own self-healing mechanism.

Reiki healing. Healers are attuned to high-frequency universal symbols. This is rather like a television set being tuned in. When you are attuned you bring in the Reiki energy to heal yourself and others.

Angel healing. This is like spiritual healing but the angels take the person who is giving healing and the person receiving it to God. The possibilities are limitless.

Natural healing. Acupuncture, homeopathy, sound healing, crystal healing, herbs, nutritional healing and most natural therapies all work to realign the sick person's energy system and clear the blockages with higher-frequency energy. They also stimulate the person's own healing powers.

All healing raises the frequency of the sick person and brings them more light. Here are steps for giving healing:

Ground yourself and your client. High-frequency energy flying about is no more useful than lightning in the sky. Light needs to be grounded to be of use. You can ground yourself by visualising roots going down from your feet into the earth. Putting your hands on someone's shoulders will also open the chakras under their feet. These are the spiritual energy centres which connect them to Earth and it will ground them. At the end of a healing it often helps to put your hands on your patient's feet.

Attune to the person you are giving healing to. This means opening your heart to them and tuning into their energy. If you offer a prayer this will have the same effect.

Ask permission from their Higher Self, even if you already have it from them.

Hold the intention of being a high and pure channel for divine healing energy to flow through you to your client. As you do this, hold a picture of their divine self which is perfect.

Detach. If you are attached to the results, you block the healing. When you finish giving healing, mentally cut yourself off from the person you are working with. This will also ensure that you do not pick up the other person's illness.

As human consciousness generally is rising now so that the higher chakras, or spiritual energy centres, are opening, more and more people are drawn to give healing. If you want to be a healer, you most certainly are one. Remember that, for the healing to be effective, your light or the light you can channel needs to be higher than that of the person you are working with. So clear your channels, set your intentions and give service as a healer.

Healing takes place because light transmutes the lower vibrations of ill health.

CHAPTER TWENTY-NINE

THE LAW OF PURIFICATION

Your aura is like a cloak around you. If your essence is pure it is a huge light surrounding and protecting you. If you have unresolved issues, they show as dirty marks. The person who is ill or in shock might have a wispy or even non-existent aura, while someone very negative would be surrounded in a dark cloak.

When your aura is totally clear and pure, no harm can befall you. No negative person or situation can get through it. Fear lets in hurt, damage or danger. Purity confers safety.

The more we evolve, the brighter the spotlight on us, so that our dark spots are revealed. When clothes are ingrained with dirt, a stain is hardly noticed. Every mark shows on clean, white clothes. People serve us by drawing attention to dirty marks on our clothing. Our auras are like our clothes.

When someone serves us by pointing out a negative spot in our aura, we call it 'pressing our buttons'. We often consider them to be difficult or challenging people. In fact they are our greatest servants.

Old resentments, angers or hurts automatically form blotches in your aura, as do any murky feelings such as envy, jealousy, pride or avarice. These dark spots will magnetise challenges into your life to draw your attention to what you need to clean up.

One way of doing an auric spot-cleanse is to write down any negative thoughts which come up. Do this with the intention of releasing them. Then burn the paper if you can. Burning transmutes the heavy energy. If you can't burn the paper, flush it down the loo because water also cleanses. Failing that, bury your paper in the earth.

Earth, fire, water and air are great purifiers. Walking in bare feet on green grass allows your negative energies to go down through your feet into the earth where Mother Earth will purify them. Being out in a breeze will clear your head and bring you back to life. Swimming, particularly in salt water in the sea, washes your aura clean. If you can't get to the sea put sea salt in your bath water.

Recently I was amazed to see someone I had not seen for ages. He had always looked world-weary and been slightly irritable. Irritability is a sure sign that your aura needs purifying. On this occasion he looked light, clear, ten years younger and full of radiant vitality. He told me that he had stopped thinking about his problems and taken up windsurfing in Devon.

Fire is probably the most powerful purifier of all. Burning old photographs, letters and belongings transmutes the negativity held in the memories and changes the psychic energy around you.

All addictions are behaviours which we repeat in order to suppress feelings. These may be overeating, compulsive spending, drinking too much alcohol or a dozen other actions. These locked-in feelings need to be released from your aura now if it is to become pure. You can use light to help you do this.

When you are about to smoke that cigarette or whatever you are about to do, pause for a moment and ask the light to support you in feeling the emotion you wish to suppress.

Ask the light to reveal to you the denied emotion.

Ask it to help you feel it.

Then ask for help in releasing it.

Finally, ask the light to heal the emotion for you.

Imagine a child who is cold and muddy, possibly even lost. A compassionate person wearing a beautiful warm cloak comes along and enfolds him in her cloak to warm him. She naturally gets mud all over her in the process. When you enfold others in your aura of love and compassion you pick up their psychic mud.

There are many people with clear auras who enfold others in their protective cloak without being consciously aware of what they are doing. Because they take on the negative energy from the other person they may feel drained or exhausted. If you have a large pure aura you do not even have to talk to someone for this to happen. Your aura permeates theirs and starts to clean it up. This means you can feel drained and tired when you are with low-vibration people. If you are in the presence of someone with a purer aura than yours, they will clean yours up.

Your aura is your buffer zone between you and the outside world. It is helpful to draw it in before you go shopping or into places where there are many people. As with all spiritual work, you draw your aura in by imagining it coming in close to your body, just as if you were drawing a cloak in tightly.

A filthy, scowling and evil-smelling person is repellent to be near. People steer clear of such a person.

Your aura has a colour, a taste and a smell. It can feel thick, smooth, light or heavy. If it is murky, smelly and full of unresolved emotions, you are sending out dark energy. Only people with similar auras will feel comfortable in your presence. Excess alcohol, cigarettes and drugs pollute your aura. Lower astral entities will happily crowd round you or live in you because your vibration matches theirs. An astral entity would feel uncomfortable in a pure aura and soon leave. If you swear, say or think unpleasant things about others, hold on to hurt, guilt or anger, feel resentful, worry and are anxious, take too little exercise, live in physical dirt or mess, eat unwholesome food and overwork, your aura will need purifying.

If you wish to walk the spiritual path, it is imperative to purify your aura so that it is clear, fragrant, light and radiant with beautiful colours. Similar high-vibration people will surround you. When you are pure and light, angels and the more evolved spiritual guides are attracted to you.

Steps to purification:
Watch your thoughts and words.
Always act with integrity.
Keep company with pure people.
Write down and burn your guilt, hurt and anger.
Forgive yourself and everyone else for everything.
Physically comb your aura out with your fingers.
Take regular exercise, preferably somewhere green or by the sea.
Ask the angels and the ascended masters to purify you.
Place the Violet Flame around you and ask your Higher Self to purify your day by blazing a trail of the Violet Flame ahead of you.
Before you go to sleep at night ask to visit Archangel Gabriel's chamber at Mount Shasta for purification.

To purify your home:
Clean and tidy your personal space.

PURIFICATION

Open the windows to let pure air flow through.

Watch less TV and pull out electric plugs when not in use.

Plants, especially ferns and spider plants, transmute heavy psychic energy.

Fill your home with spiritual books, pictures and colour.

Sing or chant sacred music.

Cleanse each room with joss sticks.

Meditate and call in the angels and Higher Beings to your home.

Your home will radiate a golden light and become a haven of love.

It is time for our planet to be purified, so that it can ascend. The ley lines which were set around the Earth in Atlantean times as an energy communication system carry a third-dimensional vibration. They are like an electricity grid which was laid underneath the surface of the earth. Some lines have broken up, others have been taken over by dark energies and a few remain pure and intact. These old ley lines need to be repaired and purified. So when you are meditating picture the ley lines of the planet whole and glowing. This old energy system is now becoming obsolete. However, it is still important for those who are not yet tuned in to the higher frequency.

The new network, which carries a fifth-dimensional fre-quency, is being laid above the earth now. Because these new lines carry a high-vibration current, it needs people with high spiritual aims and intentions to focus on them to send the energy of peace, light and inspiration along them.

The colour of the fifth-dimensional heart chakra which

is the spiritual energy centre at the heart, is pure white. This is the centre of the Christ consciousness, which is pure unconditional love, the Oneness. I was intrigued when I received guidance to ask people to start placing columns of white light wherever they are at any time. This light is to be invoked from God because the world needs to be filled with light now. The column of light will remain after you have moved away.

To purify the planet:
   Visualise light and love flowing along the network of ley lines below the surface of the Earth.
   Visualise high-frequency light and love flowing along the new network of lines above the surface of the Earth.
   Close your eyes and ask for a column of white light to come down from God, through the Universe and through you to the centre of the Earth. Visualise the column expanding and ask that anything it touches be filled and protected by the Holy Spirit. Do this, mindful that you are filling the world with the light of Christ, knowing you are preparing our planet for the coming of the Christ consciousness.

A pure aura confers total protection and draws angels towards you.

CHAPTER THIRTY

THE LAW OF PERSPECTIVE

The consciousness of the person having the experience
determines the experience.

Time is not linear. Your mental state changes your
perception of it. If you are unhappy or bored time slows
down. If you are afraid it stands still. When you feel happy,
excited and interested time flies. If I take a drive somewhere
unknown, the journey seems to take longer than when I know
the route and am relaxed.

The lower our frequency, the slower our perception of
time. People engaged in high-vibration activities find that
time passes quickly. I am told that time has speeded up on
the planet by one-third as a result of the rise in consciousness
which has already taken place.

Time can be transcended. People with certain psychic
powers can tune into past lives or into future time. When a
psychic tunes into someone's future, they are of course tuning
into a possible future. There will be several possibilities ahead
for you, depending on the free choices you make. The clair-
voyant is just seeing probabilities. Different mediums will tune
into different times in your future. All may tell you something
different and all may be correct for the period of time they
accessed. What a psychic picks up will also depend on her level
of consciousness. If a psychic can access your akashic record,
she will look at your soul choices and will be able to present
you with a more accurate assessment of your possible future.

In dreams we often move into a different time-reality. A lady told me that when she was engaged to be married, she dreamt that she was walking down the aisle alone. Her Granny, who had died, and her father were watching from above. Six weeks before the wedding her father died suddenly. Her soul gave her information from her future.

Size also depends on perception. When we are children, houses and people seem much bigger than they do to an adult. Most people have experienced going back to a childhood haunt and finding it much smaller than they expected. A mountain to a novice climber appears bigger than it does when he is experienced.

A problem which seems enormous and insurmountable in the middle of the night often appears quite manageable in the morning. The challenge is the same. Your perspective has altered.

We perceive matter as liquid, solid or gas. In reality, all is atoms and molecules moving around at different levels of density and what we see depends on our perception. Beauty is in the eye of the beholder.

The person with psychic vision who sees fairies, elves and other spirit creatures perceives a more expanded version of the Universe than does someone whose third eye is closed. Someone who is haunted by negative entities will have a very different understanding from the person who is in touch with angels and spiritual guides. The individual who has had an alien encounter or who visits other galaxies will have their consciousness expanded in a different direction. All are right in their reality. Mad people have merely accessed a different reality from that considered normal on Earth.

You will handle your challenges differently according to

your level of consciousness. For example, you are driving carefully when a young tearaway driving too fast cuts in front of you and scrapes your car. How do you respond?

If you are a third-dimensional being who walks the worldly path, you will probably curse and criticise him. You may even get out and tell him off or punch him.

A fourth-dimensional being on the path of detachment will think, 'Well, that was my karma. I obviously attracted it and it's only a tiny scrape. No point in being upset.'

The fifth-dimensional being on the spiritual path of unconditional love, which is the Christ path, gets out of the car without a thought for the damage to his own car. He is full of compassion for the young man and wants to see that he is all right. He holds the young man (and his mother) in the light.

If a client messes you about and then does not turn up for her appointment you will respond according to your perspective.

The third dimensional being will be furious, feel devalued and be angry with that client when she finally appears.

The fourth-dimensional being will detach, send a bill if appropriate and let it go.

The fifth-dimensional being will phone to see that the client is all right and talk gently to her. He will mentally thank the client for giving him free space to enjoy a walk or do other work.

Two people are assaulted. One fights all the way and nothing subdues his spirit. Another person with an abuse pattern thinks it is his fault and becomes demoralized.

A kitten is injured. The person with a closed heart sees its nuisance value and curses it. One with a compassionate heart sees its hurt and cares for it.

All depends on your perspective. There is no judgment. There is only awareness that everyone has a different reality.

If you judge something or someone it is time to reframe your perspective.

Humanity as a whole judges suicide from a third-dimensional perspective. They condemn it as wicked or weak. On the Christ path it is perceived as someone longing for more love or responding to the call to go home.

Torture can be perceived as evil or as a desire to learn compassion.

Sex can be seen as immoral or as a longing to express love.

War is terrible or an opportunity to find courage and strength.

The horrible person can be seen as a threat or as someone who is teaching you lessons. Someone who is pressing your buttons is serving you by bringing unresolved feelings to your attention. He reminds you about your own doubts.

Who knows what mission Hitler came to Earth to achieve? The person who presses the buttons of millions serves to offer lessons to all those who are affected.

Every person has a human aspect which merely masks the Divine perfection. We will continue to struggle until we see the divine flame in all people and things. Then we look at all things from a Christ perspective.

All is perfect according to God's laws. Only our perception of it is distorted. Earth is known as the plane of illusion, because nothing is as it appears to be.

View all from a perspective
of love and you will walk
the ascension pathway.

CHAPTER THIRTY-ONE

THE LAW OF GRATITUDE

Gratitude means giving thanks from your heart. When you do this, energy flows from your heart and activates certain responses from other people as well as the Universe. If you pay lip-service to gratitude or feel you ought to be thankful, your words and thoughts do not draw the same response.

A lady told me that she had never got on that well with her daughter, Maria, who was often angry with her. Furthermore, her daughter did not have much money. As she was spending Christmas with Maria, she was expecting a rather difficult and bleak holiday.

However, when she arrived on Christmas morning Maria greeted her warmly and gave her a letter to read. It was a long letter and she had decorated the borders with patterns so that it looked festive. Her daughter said she would make her a cup of coffee while she read it.

The mother sat down a little apprehensively. At first she was astonished but gradually her astonishment changed to a feeling of joy and wonder. Her daughter had written her a letter of appreciation and gratitude for all that she had ever done for her. She had filled the letter with small stories and reminiscences from her childhood.

'I cannot describe the feeling I had when I read that letter,' the mother said to me. 'My heart felt as if it would burst. I felt so loved and appreciated. It was worth more than all the presents in the world. We hugged and talked about lots of things for the first time. When I got home I felt I loved my daughter so much I wanted to give her something. I looked at my large bank balance and felt ashamed. She had gone through such a hard time and I had never wanted to give her anything before. I wrote her a big cheque and posted it with love.'

When you are totally grateful to a person for something they have done, that person feels the energy of thanks and is so overjoyed by it that they want to give you more. When you send out heartfelt thanks to the Universe for the blessings you have received, the divine energy lovingly responds by giving you even more blessings.

Heartfelt gratitude is a key to abundance. It unlocks the great resources of the Universe.

Judgment and criticism put you in hell. They are the opposite of gratitude and appreciation. If someone has done ten nasty things to you, quite likely you criticise and judge that person. You feel angry. Your body tenses. Your head aches. That is hell. There is a way out of hell to heaven. Recognise with compassion that he is a hurting person. Happy people do not do nasty things. Look for one good thing about him or one nice thing he has done for you. Focus on appreciating or being grateful for it. His attitude to you may or may not change but you will feel good again. That is heaven.

It is considered an old-fashioned concept to be grateful to your parents for giving you life. Many people still think it is their parents' fault that they were born. The truth is your spirit chose them as parents and they obliged by giving you entry to Earth and provided the circumstances and conditions, however challenging, that your soul needed for this experience.

I stayed for a few weeks in Amma's ashram in Kerala,

India. She is known as the hugging Mother because she gives everyone who comes to her *dharshan*, which is a divine blessing, by hugging them. She looks into your eyes and whispers words of love to you. Divine love pours from her into your heart centre. She is an Enlightened One, an avatar, and absolutely radiates love and tolerance. I can honestly say that I have never experienced anything like the overwhelming love she has poured into me during *dharshan*. Since she became an Enlightened One she has devoted her life to giving *dharshan* and helping to alleviate the suffering of humanity.

Apparently her childhood was horrendous. She was an unwanted girl in a large family. Furthermore, her skin was much darker than that of her parents and siblings, so she was considered a disgrace to the family. To add to that her mother took an instant dislike to her at birth and refused to protect her from the hateful vindictiveness of her oldest brother. She became a family slave, going to bed late and rising early to do the chores. She was constantly subjected to beatings and derision, not only from her oldest brother and his friends, but also from both her parents. Despite this, throughout her childhood, she danced and sang praises to Krishna. She saw God in everything and constantly called her Beloved to come to her.

One day Krishna entered her and she became enlightened. Later, the female deity entered her and she was then a fully enlightened, omniscient, omnipresent being. Soon people flocked from all over the world to receive divine love through her and a huge temple was built.

I asked one of her devotees how Amma now felt about her parents and was told that she regards them as her greatest gurus. They sit at her right hand on ceremonial days. She says that without the difficult challenges they gave her in childhood she could not have become enlightened. She is eternally grateful to them.

In personal therapy and development groups the participants are often occupied with the difficulties of their childhood. There is a tendency to focus on the negative aspects of their parents. There is a place for this in the healing process, of course, but appreciation and gratitude also heal.

I well remember one group I ran. After quite a heavy session, I asked the participants to think of positive things their parents had done for them. For a moment there was a bemused silence as their way of thinking changed direction. Then someone said, 'My mother used to make me lovely birthday cakes.' 'So did mine,' agreed another. 'I had forgotten.'

'My father used to take me fishing on Sundays.'

'Hey, my dad played football with me and really encouraged me.'

'So did mine,' came a chorus of two or three.

'My mum made me dresses with frills on.'

And so it went on. The heaviness lifted and suddenly a beautiful light energy came into the room.

The following week almost everyone shared that they had felt so much happier, more positive and healthier during the week. And they wanted to carry on remembering the positive and being grateful for it. After that we included an appreciation and gratitude slot each week. Consistently, course members reported back that parents, many now elderly, were being so much nicer to them and freely giving them the appreciation and acknowledgement they had been seeking all their lives.

Barbara had been coming to the group for a year. She was married with three children and always showed a bright, bubbly façade to the world. Underneath she was in despair. She thought she could never create a good relationship with her mother. Week after week she had expressed her frustration at how difficult her mother was and a yearning to be closer. The week after we started looking for the good in our parents and appreciating it, she told us that she had been out shopping with her mother. 'Mum was so nice, I couldn't believe it. She even bought me a dress.' She continued to appreciate her mother and be grateful for the small things she had done for her throughout her life. The following week she was delighted that her mother offered to babysit for them for the first time ever.

Appreciation is the breeze which can fan the tiniest spark into a great fire.

When you appreciate even the tiniest thing in a person or situation, it grows. As soon as you are appreciating something and being grateful for it, you are focusing on it, so by the Law of Attention, it increases and multiplies.

I heard a story about a child at school who found schoolwork difficult and became grumpy and introverted. Naturally he was unpopular. His teachers berated him as lazy, rude and difficult. He shrivelled under this judgment, criticism and condemnation. Thankfully a new teacher came to the class who understood the Laws of Appreciation and Gratitude. She devoted herself to finding something good about him or his work. It was quite difficult, but if it was possible to praise something, she did, no matter how

small. Gradually, the child's hunted look faded as he felt
safer. The teacher realised that he loved plants and flowers.
The class made a little window-box garden and he was put
in charge of it. He was praised, thanked and appreciated for
his contribution to the class. He blossomed and learnt to
smile again.

*Judgment and criticism stunt and kill flowers. Gratitude is
the sunshine which enables the petals to open up and blossom.*

When we realise that we are sent challenges because they
help us to grow, we alter our attitude to them.

It is human and understandable to be devastated at the
death of a child. I simply cannot imagine what it feels like.
I have met parents who are bitter and angry that their child
is handicapped or that their child has died. Enlightened ones
know that every child is a loan from God, a gift of love which
brings responsibilities and challenges.

Friends of mine had a very badly handicapped child who
died when he was twenty months old. They regarded the gift
of his life and death as one of the most important blessings
they had received from the Universe. They glow when they
talk about him. His short life was full of pain and operations.
It totally disrupted and changed their lives. They say he was
an angel who was sent to open them up to the spiritual path
and they are eternally grateful. They celebrate his life and
his death.

*Within every challenging situation is the gift of a lesson.
Our task is to learn the lesson and appreciate what it has
taught us.*

If you want your life to become happier, healthier and more abundant keep a gratitude journal. Every day write down a few things you are thankful for. You will find yourself looking for good things to record in it. You will automatically become more positive and appreciative. Before you go to bed rake through the cinders of the day and find the golden nuggets. Be grateful for them.

Attitudes which activate the Law of Gratitude:
　　Be positive and appreciative.
　　Count your blessings.
　　Be joyful. When you glow with happiness you are appreciating what you have.
　　Remember the good things about a person.
　　Focus on the good in every situation and person.
　　Give praise generously.
　　Use the words 'Thank you' genuinely.
　　Be loving, caring and kind.
　　Recognise your own magnificence.
　　Celebrate life and be happy.

Gratitude brings untold blessings to you.

Count your blessings and watch them multiply.

CHAPTER THIRTY-TWO

THE LAW OF BLESSINGS

When you bless someone you are invoking divine energy to touch them. When this is done with genuine intent a shaft of divine light is transferred into the person you are blessing.

In some religions priests place a hand on the head of a person as they bless them. They are activating the crown centre so that light can pass into them. This is such a powerful and personal thing to do that in many cultures it is considered bad manners to touch the crown centre.

Raising your hand in the direction of the person you wish to bless directs the blessing towards them.

In Eastern cultures a blessing is called *dharshan*. There are some avatars, those fully enlightened beings who are totally connected to God, who give *dharshan* to those who come to see them. Sai Baba has an ashram in Puttaparthi, near Bangalore in India. Sai Baba is a great avatar. His mere presence confers a blessing. Thousands flock to sit silently in his temple awaiting a glimpse of him. His message is about duty and devotion. Where it is appropriate he lifts the burdens of his devotees. As he gives *dharshan* a golden cosmic flame leaves his heart centre and enters yours. If you stay in silent meditation for twenty minutes, you keep this divine energy within you. If, however, you talk or otherwise dissipate your concentration, the cosmic flame returns to him. If you visit his ashram it is important to be mindful of this because as soon as he leaves the temple, the crowds start to chatter and rush for the exit.

They say you do not go to visit Sai Baba unless he calls

you. I first visited his ashram in 1991. Before that he had appeared to me in a few dreams or meditations but I had had no contact with his energy for some time. Then one day I was soaking in the bath when I heard a voice saying loudly and clearly, 'Come to India.' I knew it was Sai Baba and ran downstairs wrapped in a towel to look at my diary to see when I could go. I did not know where he was in India or how to get there. Next morning I had a new client. After a few minutes she said to me, 'Do you need to know how to get to Sai Baba?' In surprise, I said, 'Yes.' She said she just had a feeling I needed the information and she had it all. When it is time to visit him, he provides the means. While it is wonderful and special to sit in the energy of a Great One, you do not have to visit in your physical body. You can also call Sai Baba in during mediation and ask him for *dharshan*.

Amma, the hugging mother, whose message is love and tolerance, simply radiates light and compassion. When she gives *dharshan*, after hugging you she looks into your eyes and transfers divine energy direct into your heart. She too takes on the pain of her devotees. When I stayed in her ashram in Kerala many people, including all the ashram doctors, had eye infections. One day she decided to take the pain of everyone's infections through her body. I received *dharsan* from her in the early hours of the morning after she had been dispensing individual blessings for eight hours without a break. Her eyes were inflamed and bright red. She must have been in agony as she carried all that pain. But her smile was radiant and beautiful as if I was the first person she hugged. Sometimes we sat cross-legged on the floor of the main temple for hours waiting for our turn to go for *dharshan*. After some time my aching back used to feel as if it would break but like everyone else somehow I lasted out. After the blessing we were often allowed to sit behind her. Whenever I sat there within her aura I was totally unaware of my back. All aches, pains and stiffness dissolved. Everyone I spoke to found the same thing.

Mother Meera is another Indian avatar, who lives in Germany and gives *dharshan* from her home. I understand that her purpose in settling there is to heal the Nuremberg line and clear the dark energy left from the wars as well as spreading light through her *dharshan*. People come from all over the world to receive her silent blessing, which she offers four times a week. You enter the main room of her house and wait in silence for her to enter. Each person goes up in turn and kneels at her feet. She then places her hand on your head and as she does this she is untying your karmic knots which are held in the aura round your back. She usually transmutes between 25 percent and 50 percent of your karma. Then she looks into your eyes and nods several times. Each nod sends divine energy into you. Finally you return to your seat and meditate to absorb the divine energy.

You cannot receive a blessing from an avatar without being changed to the deepest core of your being.

When you bless your food and say thank you for it, it is filled with divine energy. Kirlian photography can film the energy of food. Much food that we eat is dead, through irradiation, chemicals, long storage and poor cooking. When blessed this food once more radiates life-force and vitality. I am not suggesting we become complacent about eating lifeless food. Eat fresh organic food wherever possible. However, blessing your food and asking the Divine to fill it with whatever nutrients you need for optimum health can help you on a physical as well as a spiritual level. There is nothing more wonderful than eating food that has had mantras sung over it during preparation and cooking, for the food is blessed.

You bless someone when they sneeze so that divine energy may enter them and they will be healthy.

Bless your work and it will increase and be filled with joy.

Bless people around you and they will be happy and fulfilled.

Bless your plants and they will grow abundantly.

Bless your home and it will be a place of peace.

Bless your body and it will become a beautiful temple for your spirit.

Here are examples of blessings you can affirm in order to change your life:

I am blessed to live in such a beautiful body.

I am blessed to be surrounded by people who love me.

I am blessed to have such a peaceful home.

Here is a wonderful food blessing:

In the name of Christ I ask that this food may be blessed so that the fruits of the earth may feed my physical body and the blessings my spiritual body.

You can also request blessings.

Bless my hands that they may serve you.

Bless my work so that it is done for the highest good.

Bless my relationships that they may be filled with love.

Bless my partner so that we may love and support each other.

Bless my children and protect and guide them.

Bless our home so that it is always filled with peace and love.

May the Divine in me bless you.

May I receive blessings from the Divine in you.

*Bless everyone and fill them
with divine energy and you
will be open to the blessings
of the Universe.*

CHAPTER THIRTY-THREE

THE LAW OF DECREE

Imagine a ladder with extending sections leaning against a skyscraper. When you are climbing the lower extensions you can see the ground, while roof and sky seem a long way away. On the lower rungs of discipleship we pray to God as supplicants, asking Him to give us what we want. Angels are the intermediaries who take the energy of our request to the Godhead.

Those who have a purely physical level of understanding are climbing this bottom section. They believe only what they can see, hear or feel and think they are separate from or even superior to others. At this level we look externally for guidance and have a limited concept of the vastness of the Universe and our place in it. This is known as living in the third dimension. On this bottom part of the ladder we make affirmations, which when repeated continually help us to change unconsciously held beliefs. Wherever we are on the ladder to ascension, prayer and affirmations are positive and valuable aids to our journey. Higher up the ladder we have greater options.

When we recognise that we are spiritual beings first, material drives become less important. We become more trusting and desire to work in co-operation with all people. No longer looking for external guidance, we follow our inner wisdom. This grants us entry to the fourth dimension and allows us to climb on to the next extension of the ladder. Our view of the Universe has considerably expanded.

THE LAW
OF
DECREE

By the time we reach the top of the fourth dimension and are preparing for our ascension initiation into the fifth dimension, we become masters. This means that we take responsibility for creating our reality. We accept that we are masters of our destiny. Therefore we are commanders. We are co-creators with the Divine. The higher we move into mastery, the more expanded our vision of creation becomes.

When we are high up the ladder, we become immensely powerful. Of course we have to accept the responsibility that goes with this. We are no longer sailors or even captains. We are commanders of the fleet. We take decisions and issue directives which everyone obeys. This is *possible* for everybody now and many are accepting total mastery of their lives. You know you are a master when you no longer blame anyone or anything for your circumstances. On a spiritual level we communicate with the spiritual hierarchy of light, consciously or unconsciously, and decide what to co-create with the Divine. A decree commands the Universe to obey our orders. As commander of the fleet everyone and everything swings into action to fulfil your orders.

When you make a decree the Universe moves to fulfil your command.

If a deckhand commands the ship without sufficient clarity or wisdom, chaos may ensue. And when we make a decree without preparation, we may not be ready for the results. Obviously a decree must be made with the greatest of integrity for the highest good of everyone.

Make it with humility, knowing that you are in service to the planet.

Command with authority and with clarity. Stand with your head up and shoulders back and say your decree aloud.

Good managing directors consult others and do background research before committing their company to a new direction. Before you commit to a decree, listen to inner guidance and outer too if necessary. Your first step is to decide very carefully what your decree is to be. Write it down, look at it from all angles, make sure that it is very positive, very clear. Consult those you trust if necessary for feedback about any flaws.

This is a formula for the wording of a decree: 'In the name of God and all that is light, I now decree . . .' Repeat this three times and then finish with, 'It is done,' or 'So be it.'

Because we do not have the overall picture while we are in a human body, it is helpful to add, 'Under the Law of Grace' or 'Under grace.' This allows the Universe to activate something different if there is a factor we are unaware of.

The decree would then be, 'In the name of God, under grace, I decree that . . . So be it.' Repeat this three times. When you have made your decree, like any director you watch the results and take all opportunities presented to you to activate your plan.

Because of its power to change our lives, a decree is tremendously exciting. It is not something to be done lightly. I have known people decree for the perfect relationship to come into their life. This sometimes results in tumult and difficulty. Everything that is stopping them from having a perfect relationship is presented to them. It all has to be faced and cleared out.

I facilitated an ascension workshop where a lady wanted to decree that a partner who loved and respected her would

come into her life. I reminded her that the outer is a reflection
of the inner and suggested that she decree that she loved and
respected herself. As soon as she made this decree she found
herself seeing a therapist who helped her to clear out the beliefs
and emotions that stopped her from loving and respecting
herself. Over the next few months different men appeared
in her life to mirror her changing beliefs. She continued to
work on herself for two years before she loved and respected
herself. Then, of course, the man for whom she had decreed
entered her life.

It is helpful to decree for qualities that we wish to have
in our life. Care is needed. If you decree for humility, you may
have to suffer humiliation in order to earn this quality. If you
decree for patience you will be offered lessons in patience. If
you decree for unconditional love, situations will be sent to
test you. Decrees, however, can offer a fast route for you to
acquire the quality that you intend to expand in your life.

We can decree for more light on Earth. If enough people
were prepared to make such decrees it would help to bring
about a happier world.

We can make decrees for the brotherhood and sisterhood
of humankind to bring the peoples of the Earth together.
When people of integrity and high spiritual values start to
decree for the highest good of everybody and everything
on earth, then the ascension of the planet and individ-
uals will take place much more quickly. The power is
ours.

Here are some examples of decrees:

'By divine Decree, in the name of God, under grace, I
invoke the Violet Flame to transmute now every negative

thought, pattern, belief, condition, attachment or alliance that I have made. It is done.' Repeat three times.

'In the name of God and all that is light, under grace, I decree that all vows made in past lives or this one which do not serve the divine plan on Earth be rescinded and released. So be it.' Repeat three times.

By divine Decree, in the name of God I now call forth a pure white column of Christ light to bring the unconditional love of Christ consciousness to Earth. It is done.' Repeat three times.

Affirmations and prayers are repeated. You make a decree once only.

When you make a decree the might of the Universe is aligned behind it.

CHAPTER THIRTY-FOUR

THE LAW OF FAITH

Faith is a quality of such high frequency that it transcends the lower laws and makes the impossible possible. Faith allows miracles to happen. Faith healing draws in God. Faith is like an unshakeable rock. It stays solid through rain, hail and mudslides. As such it confers great power.

The Law of Faith is this. If you have total faith in an outcome, it will come about. To the extent that you doubt, you allow in the possibility of failure. When you have absolute, implicit, total trust in the Divine you know that whatever is for the greatest good will happen. Faith takes away fear.

A young woman told me that she had been involved in a horrendous car crash. As the car rolled over and over she screamed in her head, 'Am I going to die?' An angel appeared to her and as its light enfolded her, she knew everything would be well. It did not matter if she lived or died. Everything was OK.

As above so below. I watched a child, laughing with joy, launching itself off a wall into its father's arms. He had absolute, implicit, total trust in his father to catch him and keep him safe. Of course his father caught him and the bond of faith which had been established was deepened. When we have innocent faith in the Divine, we will be held and kept safe.

Faith means constantly listening to your inner guidance and intuition. Blind faith is different. It implies giving away your trust without a foundation for it. The trust is misplaced through lack of discernment. Blind faith is merely hope.

I heard a story of a child whose father told him to jump off a wall and he would catch him. The child jumped and the father let him fall and hurt himself. He turned to the child and said, 'That'll teach you never to trust anyone.'

This story makes my blood run cold whenever I think about it. However, it is not about the defiling of innocence or lack of trust. I imagine that the sort of parent who would do such a thing must have had a history of unreliability. The child's trust had probably been violated many times. Undoubtedly the child *hoped* his father would catch him with very little foundation for his hope. Under spiritual, law if the child had had total faith the father would have responded by catching him.

If you build a house on insufficient foundations you will always feel a sense of uncertainty and doubt about its safety. You may be paranoid about cracks appearing because they could signal collapse. A house with solid foundations presents no such deep insecurities. You know there may be minor things to put right but the essence of the house is solid. Confidence is faith in self. If you have a foundation of self-esteem and worth you will be a relaxed and easy person to be with. No one can undermine you for you will trust your own ability and others will intuitively trust you.

Fidelity is what we call faith in a relationship. Every partnership has different ground rules about money, sex and other aspects. If you have total faith in your partner to honour your vows, you will feel secure in the relationship. Friendship too has its ground rules. If you can share an intimate part of yourself and have total faith that your friend will not laugh at you or gossip, you have a solid foundation of trust.

Faith is the foundation for success, manifestation, prayer and decrees.

When you have faith in a vision it must succeed. If you do not have enough faith, ask someone else to hold your vision for you. Their faith will ensure success.

I heard a proud father say of his successful son, 'I always knew he would succeed. I had total faith in him.'

And the son said, 'In difficult times I could hear my father's voice and knew he believed in me. It gave me the strength to continue.'

Faith moves mountains. It is the greatest power there is. If your intuition tells you something is right and you hold faith with your vision, you must succeed.

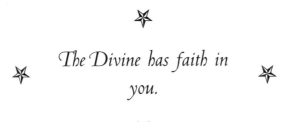

The Divine has faith in you.

CHAPTER THIRTY-FIVE

THE LAW OF GRACE

*Grace is a divine dispensation of mercy. It dissolves karma
and creates miracles. It can change matter.*

The Creator is omnipotent and radiates energy of such a
high frequency that it is beyond anything we can comprehend.
With a thought, God can end pain, illness, misery, famine and
war. But what purpose would it serve?

Our soul has accepted the opportunity to incarnate on this
planet to learn about and experience emotions and a physical
body. God has granted us free will to create our own life in
a place where every thought, word or deed manifests.

*Up to the present time we on Earth have chosen to create
famine, illness and war. We can change this by receiving and
giving grace.*

We can invoke grace to transmute our debts, change
emotional feelings, heal relationships and the physical body.
However, we must be ready to receive it. We created all our
situations with our consciousness and we must learn the lesson
before we ask for grace.

We are privileged to live on Earth at a time when there
are great avatars in physical embodiment. Avatars are divine
incarnations. They are pure undiluted divine energy and are
omniscient, omnipotent beings. They have the power to
heal through grace. However, they must regard the spiritual

laws. They will not give healing until the person has learnt his lesson.

There is a story told about Sai Baba, who is believed to be the greatest of the avatars now embodied. A mother brought her son to his ashram. The young man was handicapped and in a wheelchair. Someone asked Sai Baba why he did not heal the man. In response he showed them a picture of a past life in which the handicapped man was a very cruel judge and his mother was his assistant. They handed out incredibly savage sentences. Sai Baba said they hadn't yet learnt the lesson. He added that through caring for her handicapped son the mother was learning compassion. The man was experiencing some of the suffering he had so heartlessly inflicted on others and learning to receiving love. He said that if he healed the man neither would have learnt the lesson and both would continue to be cruel.

We can offer grace to others through our compassion, mercy, empathy, forgiveness and unconditional love. Whenever we open our hearts to another, we too receive an inflow of divine love. The more grace we offer, the more we in our turn receive.

Compassion, empathy, mercy, unconditional love and forgiveness are divine qualities which confer grace.

Every time you open your heart with compassion the love emanating from you grants someone else grace. A change of attitude may take place or the release of a deeply held fear or even a physical healing.

Forgiveness is another divine quality which dissolves and transmutes negative blocks. It results in emotional, attitudinal and physical healing taking place for both the giver and receiver.

If you lovingly and with an open heart give your last bit of food to a starving beggar you offer him grace. The food contains more than calories. It contains divine love and will nourish him at a deeper level than food alone.

Grace allows healing to occur because the high-frequency vibrations of love transmute the lower vibrations of pain and fear.

We create karma with our attitudes. All ill feeling and disputes are the karmic consequences of egotistical attitudes.

Felicity complained that her ex-husband was always horrid. One day her boyfriend said, 'It's you. You greet him crossly and you say awful things about him.' She was stunned and angry. All day she thought about it and realised her boyfriend was right. She was horrid to her ex-husband. So she sat down and really tried to understand where he was coming from. Then she wrote a long letter to him saying sorry for her attitude over the divorce and forgiving him for all the things he had done. Two days later he came round to the house and was absolutely charming and friendly. He tried to be as helpful as possible about the arrangements with the children. A total change had taken place. The interesting thing is that Felicity had never posted the letter. He felt her change in attitude and responded to it. Her forgiveness and understanding offered grace to the whole family. Everyone felt happier.

When you are ready to feel understanding and compassion or to forgive, the angels lead you to someone who can help you release your karma. This may be a therapist, herbalist, chiropractor, allopathic doctor or healer. It may be the person next door or someone who can speak words of wisdom. It may be a book or television show which totally transforms your attitude. The moment you are ready, you will be placed where you can heal.

I am sometimes asked if doctors and natural healers are working to repay their own karma or whether they have completed their karmic repayments and are now offering grace to others. People are very often drawn to a particular healing profession for their own healing and to enable them to complete karma. It is the open-hearted offering of their skills that transmutes their karma and at the same time offers grace to others. I like to think that many in the caring and healing professions are now purely dispensing grace.

Healers are channels through which high-frequency vibrations may pass. They are instruments of grace.

Angels work with grace, constantly whispering to us to think, do or say that which will dissolve our karma. They try to help us to forgive others or make decisions for our highest good, so that we are living in the light.

We have always been able to ask Source for grace to forgive our sins and dissolve a backlog of karmic debt. However, because we are living at such an incredible time of evolution of our souls, there is at present a divine amnesty in place. This means that grace is being granted more readily than before. Nevertheless, we have to be deemed ready to receive it. So if you have done everything possible to resolve a situation or a relationship, call on the Divine for grace and it may well be granted. You can help to bring grace to our planet.

The more you open your heart to welcome strangers, to let go of anger or care for the sick and senile, the more grace pours into the planet. Every time you pray for another or help someone with love, the planet becomes more filled with light.

Give and receive grace
which is the divine mercy
that sets people free.

CHAPTER THIRTY-SIX

THE LAW OF ONE

If you fly above the clouds there is only glorious sunshine.
Below the clouds there is shadow and light. In heaven there is
only light. On Earth we experience dark and light. This is the
duality which comes from the free will which we experience
on Earth. Beyond the fifth dimension there is only light.
Wherever we are, all is perfect. Everything is God and we
are all part of God. Duality is merely a learning experience
to expand our light.

If a deeply loving married couple is separated by physical
distance there is in reality no separation. They are connected
by every thought and longing. Life offers us an illusion that
we are separate from God in order that we may learn how
truly one we are.

*In the fifth dimension there is only one spiritual law. We
are all one. We are all part of God.*

This means that I am a Christian, a Hindu, a Buddhist,
a Moslem, a Jew, a Sikh.

I am black, brown, yellow, white.

I am male and female.

I am homosexual, heterosexual.

I am animal, vegetable, mineral.

I am rich. I am poor.

I am human. I am divine.

There is no differentiation. All is one.

Imagine a carpet of exquisite, intricate design and glowing colours. The threads are all the same but the colours different. Each colour plays its part. Dark highlights light. It is the differences in colour and texture which make the tapestry of life so exciting.

You are an important thread in that carpet, a part of the whole.

A third dimensional being fears the differences between the races and the sexes and all of creation. When you know we are all one, you honour the differences.

In the fifth dimension the law is, 'Do as you would be done by.' If a thread of the carpet is damaged, the whole is diminished. If a thread is enhanced, so is the whole. Whatever you do to another you are ultimately doing to yourself.

Before you act take a moment to think, 'How would I feel if this was done to me?' You may want to make different choices.

If you would like someone to pick up the piece of litter in your front garden, pick up the sweet wrapper that has blown into theirs.

I was making improvements to my house and putting much money and effort into it. I said to my daughter Lauren, who is a very wise soul, 'What's the betting I move house now?'

She replied, 'Surely the aim is to leave your house as you would like to find your next home?'

She is right. I thanked her for the reminder. After that I really enjoyed beautifying my home, knowing that everything I do for myself I am doing for the whole.

Everyone is on their own path back to Source. Who are we to judge the route another is taking? Our task is to do our best. However, we must also recognise and honour our own humanness. We are unlikely to be perfect while on the Earth plane.

If you constantly criticise or find fault with a child, you will never know his magnificence. If you repeatedly tell your dog off, he will be a miserable creature. If you are self-critical your light will shine less brightly than it could do. When you accept all creatures and honour the divinity in them, they will blossom and so will you.

Like all aspiring spiritual beings I aim to walk my talk and inevitably I make mistakes. I remember talking to my guide on one occasion about this. He said, 'You are constantly criticising yourself and feeling bad if you are teaching something that you have not incorporated into your life. We are telling you that it is *the part of you that has mastered the lesson* which is bringing the teaching through. Relax and be kind to yourself.'

> *The Law of Oneness is about accepting everyone*
> *and everything as they are, without judgment. This*
> *includes yourself.*

The protective barriers we put up to defend ourselves prevent us from being one with others. You can never get close to a very defended person. It is only when someone shares something of themselves that you feel close. We are asked to start taking down our separating barriers now, for as much as we are closed off from others, we are closed off from God.

Dogma creates rigid constructs and walls. They are part of the Old Age that is coming to an end.

Secrets keep us behind walls. At this time now the skeletons are coming out of cupboards. It is a strange thing how our own secrets feel so terrible. To someone else they are not so bad. A secret shared is a wall dissolved.

You are the light of the world. Nothing can diminish the wonder of your light. Only walls can hide it away. Seek your own light within and look for the light in others.

When we are one, we do not need walls to separate us.

The new spirituality is about creating bridges. When we live the Law of One we create bridges by looking for the commonality in religions, peoples and in disputes.

Inasmuch as you hurt any part of God's creation, you hurt yourself and you hurt God. Just as you are invited to be here for this learning on Earth, so are animals, insects, trees and plants. All are learning and evolving. They are our younger brethren. If you despoil the earth, you damage the whole of creation. However, you are entitled to your space just as an animal is entitled to his territory.

So if your kitchen is overrun by ants, what do you do? First you talk to the Higher Self or the oversoul of the ants and remind them that this is your territory. You ask them to move to a log in the garden or a tree on the pavement where they will be safe. If they ignore two warnings, tell them that you will have to return them to the light if they do not honour your space. If they are outside your house then you do not have the right to kill them. Honour trees and plants by telling them with a thought that you are about to prune them. Act with harmlessness.

When you understand the Law of One, you accept your

own divinity. You start listening to your intuition, rather than seeking answers externally. You become a co-creator with God.

On Earth we tend to separate good and bad, dark and light. Yet darkness serves the light. It is your servant and your teacher. When you recognise this, you move beyond duality to oneness.

A mother who loves her child helps it to grow up. She knows that within the child is an embryo adult, who merely has to experience and grow to reach mature status. Like that child, you are here to experience and grow. Your spirit is divine and like the mother is showing you the way.

Oneness is accepting your own divinity.

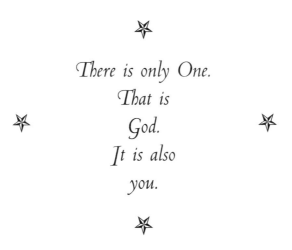

There is only One.
That is
God.
It is also
you.

For more details of Diana Cooper's books, tapes and workshops, visit her website at www.dianacooper.com

NEALE DONALD WALSCH

CONVERSATIONS WITH GOD BOOK I
An Uncommon Dialogue

'Contains a wisdom I believe we all have inside us but don't stop
to listen to' Dr Bernie Siegel

Suppose you could ask God the most puzzling questions about exist-
ence — questions about love and faith, life and death, good and evil.
Suppose God provided clear, understandable answers.
It happened to Neale Donald Walsch.

It can happen to you.

You are about to have a conversation . . .

Walsch was experiencing a low point in his life when he decided
to write a letter to God, venting his frustrations. What he did not
expect was a response. As he finished his letter, he was moved to
continue writing — and out came these extraordinary answers to
his questions.

They will amaze you with complex paradoxes that make perfect
sense, profound logic, and astounding truths. Here are answers that
bring together as one the deeper meaning of all beliefs and traditions.
Here are answers that will change you, your life, and the way you
view other beings.

For those with an open mind, a limitless curiosity, and a sincere
desire to seek the truth, this book is stunning.

HODDER AND STOUGHTON PAPERBACKS

ROBERT HOLDEN

HAPPINESS NOW!

Timeless Wisdom for Feeling Good *Fast*

'I love this book! If you want to embrace a more powerful and fulfilling way of being in this world, then immerse yourself in *Happiness Now!*' Susan Jeffers

'In a world filled with ghastly suffering and sorrow, Robert Holden's book *Happiness Now!* is a reservoir of deep nurturing joy . . . I consider this book a true gift and hope that millions will read it' John Bradshaw, author of *Creating Love*

Happiness Now! is a truly powerful journey of exploration and insight into one of life's most treasured goals. It offers a message of profound hope and healing.

Robert Holden gives a hugely personal, warm and entertaining account of the key insights and experiences that led him to develop his pioneering work into happiness, love and success. Radical and compassionate, challenging and helpful, visionary and practical, *Happiness Now!* shows the keys to emotional healing, true self-acceptance, loving relationships, inner confidence, and pure peace of mind.

HODDER AND STOUGHTON PAPERBACKS

CHUCK SPEZZANO

IF IT HURTS, IT ISN'T LOVE
Secrets of Successful Relationships

'Chuck Spezzano's work is not only spiritual and inspirational, it's also immensely practical ... His books are full of wisdom and no-one can fail to learn and develop from his teaching' Virginia Ironside, *Sunday Mirror*

If it Hurts, it isn't Love is a simple, but life-transforming collection of over 350 principles that help heal the problems and hurt in relationships. Inspiring and full of heartfelt guidance and encouragement, this book shows us how to look at the world afresh, in a way that heals pain and brings love and forgiveness.

With over 28 years' experience as a Doctor of Psychology and teacher, Chuck Spezzano gives you the tools you need to transform your relationships. Going beyond common wisdom to new realms of insight, *If it Hurts, it isn't Love* will bring everyone the love and happiness they deserve.

HODDER AND STOUGHTON PAPERBACKS